REMEMBERING

WOODSTOCK

R E M E M B E R I N G

WOODSTOCK

FROM THE PUBLICATIONS & ARCHIVES OF THE
HISTORICAL SOCIETY OF WOODSTOCK

RICHARD HEPPNER, EDITOR

Charleston · London

THE
History
PRESS

This early map of Woodstock illustrates portions of the original Hardenburg Patent purchased by Robert Livingston.

R. GREEN Co.

SHUES LAKE

J. Burke
P. C. Burke
J. Burke

Overlook Mountain
J. E. Lasher's House
or
Woodstock Mountain

A. Lockwood

C. B.
Saw Mill

A. Dubois
W. Dubois

D. Woolven

J. McMurdy

J. McMurdy

E. Taylor
Bear

C. B.

Miss Scribner

E. Taylor

E. McDonald

E. McDaniel

R. McDonald

G. Mead

Mountain Home

E. Snyder

J. F. Russell
J. Gabriel
Mead
E. Balt
U. Livingston

P. Murrey
McMurry

J. C. Lewis
E. B.

J. Fiero

J. Woolven

J. Mayer Nº 22

G. Mayer

J. W. Rose

A. Griner

Nº 9
DIST.

Nº 6
DIST.

Quarries

H. Vosburgh

J. E. L.
Saw Mill
Miller
Saw Mill
Reynolds & Elting

H

J. Daly
J. Risley

J. Spencer
Lewis

SCHOOL
Nº 22

C. H. Krack
S. Ricks

D. Ricks

J. Risenberg

H. Hogan

C. B.

P. Stall
A. Risley

Mrs. Cashdollar
T. Hennessy
W. H. Kunezes
Shultis

Vandebogart
C. Ricks
McRisley

F. D. Harder
W. Cole

A. Lewis
J. Risley

C. Beaty

H. Fingar

E. D. Harder

J. Johnson
Taylor

J. Happy

WOODSTOCK P.O.

Quarry

W. Lasher
L. Van Dasbeck

Lasher
P. J. Harder
A. Risley
J. Lasher

J. Ricks
J. Johnson

CEM.
Hasbrouck

U. Short

W. Lasher

J. Riley
Parsonage

LUTH. CH.
J. G. L.

R. Van Etten

E. J. Wolven

SCHOOL
Reynolds

Saw Kill

J. Riley

J. Crane

Tannery

SCHOOL
C. Dick

J. Lowther

C. Disch

J. Smith
E. Mann
S. Smith

J. A. Kiersted

J. A. Nash

DIST.

Nº 3

S. Yerry

E. Riley

J. R.

B. Degraff

F. E. Gray
J. Bonesteel
Lasher

E. Bonesteel

J. R.

J. Jones
L. Herrick
J. Bonesteel

Nº 2

J. G. L.

ST.

DIST.

Nº 2

KINGSTON

J. Grim

Published by The History Press
Charleston, SC 29403
www.historypress.net

Front cover image: *Overlook Mountain from Allen's Hill*, by Willard Allen, oil on canvas. *From the collection of Donald Allen.*
Back cover image: *Photo courtesy of the Historical Society of Woodstock.*

All images courtesy of the Historical Society of Woodstock Archives unless otherwise noted.

First published 2008

Manufactured in the United States

ISBN 978.1.59629.482.0
Library of Congress Cataloging-in-Publication Data

Remembering Woodstock : from the archives and publications of the Historical Society
of Woodstock / edited and written by Richard Heppner.
p. cm.
ISBN 978-1-59629-482-0
1. Woodstock (N.Y.)--History--Sources. 2. Woodstock (N.Y.)--Social life and customs--
Sources. 3. Artist colonies--New York (State)--New York--History--Sources. 4. Woodstock
(N.Y.)--Biography. 5. Historical Society of Woodstock (Woodstock, N.Y.)--Archives. I.
Heppner, Richard R. II. Historical Society of Woodstock (Woodstock, N.Y.)
F129.W85R46 2008
974.7'34--dc22

2008037253

A meeting of the Historical Society of Woodstock in 1931, two years after its founding.

This book is dedicated to the many volunteers of the Historical Society of Woodstock who, throughout the years, have kept the history of Woodstock alive and well. It is also dedicated to the citizens of Woodstock and to the spirit of independence and creativity that has sustained our community.

CONTENTS

ACKNOWLEDGEMENTS

A s with any endeavor, this work could not have been completed without the generosity of a number of people. I would like to thank the Town of Woodstock for its continued support of the Historical Society of Woodstock. Thanks also go to Tinker Twine, Jeremy Wilber, Jonathan Simcosky of The History Press, the *Woodstock Journal* and the *Woodstock Times*. Thanks also to Jean White and Deborah Heppner for their proofreading efforts. Finally, grateful appreciation goes to the citizens of Woodstock, whose history this is. May our future be as glorious as our past.

Board of Directors—The Historical Society of Woodstock

Deborah Heppner, President
Weston Blelock, Vice-president
Renee Kristol, Treasurer
Kathy Anderson, Secretary
JoAnn Margolis, Archivist
Jean White, Volunteer Services
Richard Heppner, Woodstock Town Historian

All proceeds generated by this work by the Historical Society of Woodstock go directly to support the society's programs.

INTRODUCTION

By Richard Heppner, Woodstock Town Historian

Passed the 11th of April, 1787

Whereas in and by a law of this State entitled "An act for increasing the number of assessors throughout the State," it is enacted and declared, that as well as for the purpose of assessments, as all military purposes whatsoever, the settlements of Woodstock and Great and Little Shandaken, in the county of Ulster, should be thereby severally annexed to, and made parts of the township of Hurley: And whereas the inhabitant of the same respective settlements by their petition have represented to the legislature, that they live remote from other inhabitants, and have no town officers to regulate the roads, or to compel any persons to work on them; and that they are subject to other inconveniences, by means whereof other persons are discouraged from settling among them: and thereupon praying to be erected into a district, in their said petition described and named; and it appearing to the legislature reasonable that the prayer of the said petition be complied with. Therefore,

Be it enacted by the people of the State of New York, represented in Senate and Assembly, and it is hereby enacted by the authority of the same, That so much of the same three settlements of Woodstock, and Great and Little Shandaken, as is contained in the boundaries herein after described, shall be, and hereby erected into a separate township, by the name of the township of Woodstock.

Governing bodies rarely foresee the enduring consequences of their actions. Which is why, when the New York legislature passed the preceding act on April 11, 1787, those gathered in New York State's capitol that day could be forgiven for not comprehending the course of events they had just set in motion. To be sure, some of those occupying seats in New York's central government at the time—men with names such as Hamilton and Clinton— could be forgiven for their lack of curiosity. No doubt their attention was focused not on what Albany was doing that spring, but rather on the actions of those gathered in Philadelphia in pursuit of a national constitution. Nonetheless, one wonders if men who had the ability to foresee the creation of a new nation conceived in liberty possessed the slightest interest as to where their actions that day might lead? Truth be told, there is little in the record to indicate that they gave it a second thought. After all, Woodstock was just another small town in a remote section of New York's Catskill Mountains.

In fact, as the birth of this new town paralleled the birth of a new nation, there were few outward signs that distinguished the town of Woodstock from other towns similarly existing across the state of New York. Save for the fading presence of Indian hunters, a few hand-hewn structures, powerful mountain streams and an abundance of hemlock forests, there was little to indicate that Woodstock would rise to be a different sort of town. That it would produce and attract a people contrary to the nature of central authority while, at the same time, quite fond of the freedoms that same central authority had codified into the law of the land. That it would become a town where the physical environment would seemingly merge with those who would inhabit the land to produce an individuality that would navigate a unique road through the nineteenth century while giving birth to an explosion of creativity in the twentieth. In these, and in many other ways, the town that was voted into existence on that April day would rise from the remote mountainsides to eclipse the lives of many who served as midwives to its creation.

To understand the one constant in the history of Woodstock, visitors and natives alike need only to gaze upward toward the gentle slopes of Overlook Mountain. For it is in that gentle face that they will find the beacon that has summoned the unique individualism and the creative spirit that grace the pages of Woodstock's story.

Like many small towns across the Northeast, Woodstock's early history is one of individual struggle in an effort to sustain a simple existence. Prior to the arrival of the first white settlers in the mid-1700s, Indian hunters once traversed the trails along the Sawkill Creek to reach the Overlook

Throughout the town's history, Overlook Mountain has stood at the center of Woodstock life. *Photo by Richard Heppner.*

hunting grounds that sustained settlements to the south. As both Dutch and English settlers made their way up the Hudson River, the first white settlers arrived to coax crops from Woodstock's rocky soil and craft a living from the forests and mountain streams that surrounded them. By the 1800s, however, the economic focus of settlers shifted to more industrial ends. In 1809, the first glass factory was built in the hamlet of Shady. By the 1830s, tanning, which required a plentiful water supply and tannic acid obtained from hemlock trees, found both resources in abundant supply in Woodstock. When both industries struggled to sustain themselves, Woodstockers turned to quarrying bluestone by the mid-1800s in an effort to meet the demands of urban expansion in cities along the eastern seaboard. Later in the century, as Woodstock was discovered as a place where city dwellers could find respite and comfort away from the unhealthy air of an urban summer, Woodstockers learned to craft a living not from the land itself, but from what others saw in the land.

A truly transformative chapter in Woodstock's history began in 1902 when, on a spring day, a man by the name of Bolton Brown emerged from the thicket near the summit of Overlook Mountain and first viewed Woodstock and the expanse below. Hired by Ralph Whitehead to seek a physical location that would match Whitehead's vision for an art colony, Brown, upon beholding the vista before him, wrote of that moment, "Exactly here the story of modern Woodstock really begins." With the founding of Whitehead's Byrdcliffe art colony, the arts had arrived in Woodstock. In addition to Byrdcliffe, Hervey White would go on to establish the Maverick Art Colony in 1905, while the Art Students League would set up operations in Woodstock a year later.

It was the continuation of that same creative spirit that would ultimately transform Woodstock once again. While music had long been a part of the Woodstock arts scene, something quite unique began to emerge in the 1960s that would, ultimately, lend the name of Woodstock to an entire generation. The names, of course, are now legendary—Dylan, Hendrix, The Band—to note but a few. And, as their music echoed up and down Tinker Street, it also summoned young people and members of the counterculture to begin their own journey to Woodstock. Though the Woodstock Festival wasn't actually held here, the spirit and the energy that it gave birth to were certainly conceived here.

In today's post-9/11 world, the face of Overlook Mountain continues to draw newcomers and visitors alike. In doing so, it extends the same promise that it offered both Native Americans and early settlers more than two centuries ago. For within the shadow of Overlook, the individual is always welcome and new and creative beginnings are always possible.

These are the stories of those beginnings, as compiled by the Historical Society of Woodstock. Founded in 1929, the society, under the initial leadership of its president, Martin Schutze, understood the importance of maintaining a permanent record of Woodstock's history. More than most, Schutze recognized the unique change that had transformed Woodstock from a rural, agricultural town into what we now proclaim as the "colony of the arts." At the same time, and ever cognizant that no one era can exist unhinged from the whole, Schutze saw the need for the generations of the present to chronicle the totality of Woodstock's story. That vision manifested itself in a remarkable series of booklets titled *The Publications of the Historical Society of Woodstock*. Culled from that collection, the stories that follow represent the unique elements of Woodstock's story. Each, on its own, offers an important link in the totality that the founding members of the society sought to represent. From the early "pioneering" days to the establishment of one of the premier art colonies in the nation, these are the stories of one of America's most famous small towns.

A final note: preserving local history is a job that often rests on the shoulders of volunteers. It falls to dedicated individuals who understand that

PUBLICATIONS of the WOODSTOCK HISTORICAL SOCIETY

July 1933   No. 10

CONTENTS:

A 1933 publication of the Historical Society of Woodstock.

The village of Woodstock within the shadow of Overlook Mountain, circa 1920.

each story they examine and preserve represents an important building block in the grand foundation that becomes our national story. More often than not, these stories center on individuals, families and events unique to small towns. It is through their efforts, through the vantage point of local history, that we come to understand that the collective past is but an accumulation of our singular stories—unique in their own telling, but each inexplicably intertwined with our notion of community. Further, we also comprehend how each story shapes, and is shaped by, the physical environment in which it unfolds and that the lives our families and ancestors have crafted cannot be disassociated from that landscape we call home. In many respects, through our pursuit of local history, we arrive back where we began. And, in doing so, we come to understand that we are not separate from our past, but are an integral part of a combining experience known as community.

PIONEER LIFE IN WOODSTOCK

By Louise Hasbrouck Zimm

Editor's Note: The following essay was originally written and presented to a gathering of the Historical Society of Woodstock in 1930. Later that year, it was included within the 1930 edition of the Publications of the Historical Society of Woodstock. *Some portions have been edited to better accommodate the written page. Spelling used in the original documents cited by Zimm has not been altered. Throughout the essay, the reader will note references to "Sylvester." Here, the author is referring to Nathaniel Bartlett Sylvester's* History of Ulster County, New York, *with illustrations and biographical sketches of its prominent men and pioneers, originally published in 1880. The "Livingston" referred to by the author is Robert Livingston of New York's notable Livingston family. Livingston ultimately obtained the largest portion of the original Hardenburg Patent, which included the land that was to become Woodstock.*

We are all gathered here tonight because we are interested in Woodstock history; but I imagine there is one question that is bothering a good many of us. That is, has Woodstock a history?

I would like to answer that by asking some other questions. If you had been captured by Indians led by a Tory neighbor on the Woodstock-Saugerties road, returning from church service; if you had been taken on that long, long trail through the woods and along the lakes and rivers to Montreal, kept in a British prison two years and escaped by the help of an Indian whom you had known at home; got back finally after terrific hardships and, meeting the Tory, your betrayer, in the local grocery, said something to him about letting bygones be bygones—wouldn't you have felt that you had lived through a bit of history? I think that probably Peter Short and Peter Miller, to whom this happened during the Revolution, felt that they had. Or if you had crept into dens to shoot at the blazing eyes of panthers; if you had leaned out of your bedroom window in the moonlight to pick off the wolves that were killing your flock of sheep; if you had felled the logs to build the house in your mountain clearing, had watched the giant hemlocks crash so that their bark could be used in the tanneries; had seen the glass factories appear and then vanish like huge fireflies in the remotest spots of the mountain, as far up as Mead's; if you had heard the cow horns blowing, the tin pails clattering and shots fired in the Down Rent War, after hundreds of men dressed as Indians had paraded in a great Snake-Around in the valley near Wittenberg to frighten the "Tories," that is, the agents and those who took the side of the Livingstons in their efforts to retain a kind of feudal patroonship with their system of three-life leases; if you danced with the Irish quarrymen in the pine woods at Lewis Hollow, when that lately almost deserted locality was a flourishing village of 150 people; if you'd watched Jerry Leyendecker's four-horse stage from the Overlook Mountain House dash down the village street of Woodstock and come to a dramatic dead stop at the Brinkerhoff House, and from it, say, General Grant had alighted; why, then, you might feel that Woodstock had a history.

But—I want to make one thing perfectly plain—Woodstock was not the village Rip Van Winkle lived in! There is nothing whatsoever to show that Washington Irving had us in mind, and what's more, none of the natives ever claimed that he had. This is a circumstance, I feel, that gives us a certain originality among Catskill villages. Also, though Woodstock dates from the time of the Revolution, there is no house here in which General Washington is supposed to have slept, and no old lady who claims to have danced with Lafayette. And so, whether this is our native place or our chosen home, the home of our hearts, we can feel that it is a unique spot, one we can be proud of and one whose history is anything but common.

First Settlers

When and by whom was Woodstock settled? The first settler here is said by all the histories to have been Philip Bonesteel, who arrived in 1770 and cleared land about a mile below Woodstock village. According to the histories, there were no more settlers until 1776, when Edward Short took up land in Yankeetown. But it may be that the histories have omitted something here, for an examination of the Kingston Dutch Reform Church records for early Woodstock marriages show that two young men, Peter Hans and Frederik Kittel, who took brides in 1785, give their place of birth as Woodstock. Both Wilhemus Reistler and Annatje Sneider, who were married to each other in 1790, were born (according to the records) in Woodstock. Assuming that Hans and Kittel were at least fifteen, and Wilhemus Reistler and Annatje Sneider not much under twenty when married, their families must have been living in Woodstock in or near 1770; so that perhaps the early population was larger than is supposed, and Philip Bonesteel did not live out here for many years in solitary glory. We do know for certain that a few years after the Revolution, about 1788, a whole influx of families took up their abode in Woodstock township. They were good families, practically every one of them, of fine Holland Dutch, French Huguenot, German Palatine, English, Scotch or Irish stock; and the members of them who came out here to settle were, I feel, at least as energetic, clever and enterprising as any they left behind. I have no doubt that the other early settlers were equally fine men, and as for the women who had the courage to come out with them, I will not even attempt to speak their praise.

Woodstock pioneer life must have been the same as in all frontier communities: first came the clearing of the land for agriculture, and then the building of mills, for which the Sawkill and Beaver Kill furnished abundant water power. Jacob Montrose is said to have built the first gristmill, and Robert Livingston the first sawmill. The pioneers were also busy laying out roads. The first highway, surveyed in 1788 and laid out by Petrus Short and William Snyder, was four rods wide and ran from the bounds of the corporation of Kingston to Lake Hill. The survey, as quoted by Sylvester, shows a sawmill, bridge, gristmill and high bridge over the Sawkill in Woodstock. It also mentions the houses of Michael Berger, David Kool, Wm. Snyder, Robert Bessay, Philp Peck, Andries Riselar, Cornelius DeMond, Ephraim Van Keuren, Hendrick Plass, Edward Short and Frederick Rowe.

EARLY INDUSTRIES

One of Woodstock's very first industries was inn keeping. From earliest times to the present day—very much to the present day—those desiring to improve their fortunes in our locality have turned to boarding or feeding the paying guest. Therefore it is not incredible, though a trifle surprising, to find that as early as 1789, two years after the town was founded, seven tavern licenses were granted for the sum of eight shillings apiece. One wonders how so many inns could have flourished at this early date. I suppose the explanation lies in the rough conditions of the roads, which made traveling so difficult that farmers taking grain to mill, lumbermen, people going to visit their families in the older settlements and back to Kingston and Saugerties to be married or have their children baptized needed rest and refreshment at frequent intervals along the way. And there was plenty of the latter to be had, and cheap, too, whether it was paid for in kind (as their Dutch forebears paid by a schepel of wheat for a pint of brandy) or in English shillings and sixpences, French or Spanish coins, all of which were in circulation. Inn keeping must have been profitable, and the profession became so crowded that by 1814 or earlier the Commissioners of Excise were obliged to take the following oath:

> *I do solemnly swear in the presence of Almighty God that I will not on any account or pretence whatsoever grant any license to any person within the said town of Woodstock for the purpose of keeping an inn or tavern except when it shall appear to me to be absolutely necessary for the benefit of traveler; and I will in all things while acting as a Commissioner of Excise, do my duty according to the best of my judgment and ability without fear, favor or partiality to it.*

Perhaps sometime one of our artists will make a pictorial map of early Woodstock, using for a basis the old road surveys, which show the location of the early roads, houses, mills and factories. For instance, we learn from them that there was a schoolhouse in 1808. Also that the glass factories, Woodstock's most picturesque early industry, were established sooner than most of us had supposed. Our immediate locality was really a pioneer in the industry in New York State. Two glass manufacturers, the Woodstock Glass Manufactory and the Bristol Glass House (Bristol was the old name for Shady), are mentioned in a survey of 1809; the same survey speaks of the road of the Old Glass House, showing that one factory, probably up the mountain, had already been started and abandoned. There was still another glass factory, called the New York Crown Cylinder Glass Manufacturing Co., in Woodstock in 1833, for we find John Holland deeding them a "certain lot or parcel of potatoes now in the ground…and one white sow two years old last spring and one yellowish red calf" at that date. Then there is the Ulster Company, mentioned on the deeds of land in Lewis Hollow and vicinity, which residents believe to be the same that built the Glasco Turnpike. These factories made window glass, domes to go over clocks and ladles; also occasionally small objects, such as alligators. These may have been made by the workmen with what was left of the "metal" after the day's work was done, for their own use, as was the custom in other early factories. It is to be hoped that the society may be able to collect some of this local glass, at least for a loan exhibit, if not for a permanent one. And, by the way, are there any windowpanes in old houses showing the "bull's eye," or lump by which the sheet of glass was attached to the pontil iron, in the old-fashioned method of glass blowing? These panes, once despised for lack of transparency, would now be highly prized. They were usually put in transoms or skylights.

EARLY LAWS

When the town officers met every year at William Boyd's in Shandaken, or Elias Hasbrouck's or William Eltinge's or Newkirk and De Forest's or some other convenient place, one of their chief duties was to pass or re-pass the bylaws about cattle and other animals, which occur in practically the same language from year to year.

"Resolved, that a Ram shall not be suffered to run at large unhampered from the first day of September ensuing until the fifteenth of November under the penalty of the owner of said Ram and fleece to the person who may take him up and Confine him without any undue advantage." (1809)

"Resolved that every person or persons in the said (town) of Woodstock who shall ketch Crows within the Said Town in the month of May and June now ensueing shall be intitled for everyone or more the sum of Six Cents to be paid by the Town Clerk of said town as soon as the money shall be paid into his hands by the Collector for that purpose. And four cents for every ground Squirl all of which must be brought to the house of the Town Clerk in said town within twenty five hours after catch."

"Voted and resolved that a hog of one year old Shall be a lawful Commoner after yoaked with a Croach yoak of 6 inches long and a good Ring in his nose and so in proportion for Older and younger." (1805)

"No cattle shall be allowed to run at large during the winter season." (1823)

"Also that Every Tavern Keeper Shall not allow any fowls to haunt Sleighs or Wagons about his Shed or yard. Any person finding fowls as above shall be allowed to Kill the same & Delivered to the landlord."

"Also that every person who shall allow his Hogs to run at large at any public Place where people resort shall pay a fine of 25–100 for each Hog & the Damage any person may receive."

"Also that there be Seventy five Cents bounty on every fox."

In 1824, sheep were declared no free commoners in the town of Woodstock, and "all cattle suffered to run at Large in the commons of the Town from other Towns Shall suffer a fine of five dollars a head if taken by the Inhabitants of this town and put in their charge."

In 1834, it was voted lawful for the "owners and possessors of Horses and Cattle in the Town of Woodstock to let them run or go at large on the Highways in Months of April, May, June, July, August, September, October and November."

According to the Supervisors' Record, from 1830 to 1874, the last wolves in the township were killed in 1829 by Moses Eccent, and in 1830 by D.M. Hasbrouck. They were for each paid fifteen dollars. From that time on, no more wolf bounties seem to have been paid, and one can hardly believe that a farmer who had killed a wolf would have omitted to collect the bounty. Fox bounties have been paid right along to date.

THE POOR AND EARLY SLAVES

There was a curious state of affairs in early days in regard to the poor, for whom provision was made by the town from the first year of settlement. This provision varied from a very small sum to $200, and it was expended in the following manner. I quote from the town records, omitting names for obvious reasons.

> Peter C. and his wife Erriet having become paupers of the said Town and was sot up at vendue the annual Town meeting which was held in April the 7, 1818 and was struck of on the Lowest Bider which was Peter W. for Eleven dollars a month to be maintained in Sickness and in health and in Clothing for one year.
>
> Hannah H. the wife of Joshua H. has become chargeable to the said Town and was sold at Public Vendue on the 27th of June 1818 to the lowest Bider which was William W. for nine dollars and fifty Cents Per Month to be maintained in Sickness and in Health till next annual Town Meeting in April 1819.

These "sales" of paupers occurred until about 1826, when they seem to have ceased, or at least disappear from the records. Such methods were practiced also in other places in the eastern states at about the same period. One of the first surveys of the treatment of the poor in this country, the

Early "Record of the Poor," as maintained by the town of Woodstock.

Yates report, published in 1824, says: "The poor are sold at auction; the meaning of which is that he who will support them becomes their keeper; and it often happens, of course, that the keeper is himself almost a pauper before he purchases, and adopts this mode in order not to fall a burden upon the town. Thus he and another miserable human being barely subsist upon what would hardly comfortably maintain himself alone." The paupers in Woodstock belonged to two families, who appear in the records every year, the old people disposed of as described, and the children first "sold" and then indentured, until they were probably all placed in the world. One of the H. family was indentured as follows: (The form of words is very old. A similar indenture is quoted by Alice Morse Earle in *Colonial Days in Old New York*, dated 1719, with the note that it was used in much earlier times.)

Andrew H. a Poor Child of the said Town & likely to Become Chargable to the same Being of the age of Fourteen years and Seven Months is bound as an apprentice to Robert E. Carman of the Town of Hurley in sd Co. wheelwright him to serve until the said apprentice shall attain to the age of twentyone years during all which time the said apprentice his said master faithfully shall serve his Secrets keep & his lawful command obey he shall do no damage to his Master nor see it done by others without giving him notice thereof he shall not waste his masters goods or lend them unlawfully away he shall not contract Matrimony in the said term at cards Dice or any unlawful game he shall not Play nor absent himself night or day from his Masters Service during the said term without his Leave but in all things behave himself as a faithful apprentice ought to do during the time aforesaid & the said Robert W. Carman doth hereby for himself his executors & administrators covenant and agree...that he will Teach & Instruct the sd apprintice in the art in a trade of a wagon maker & a Shop Joiner according to the Best of his ability and during the time aforesaid provide & allow the said apprintice sufficient Meat Drink apparel lodging washing and all necessary accommodations for an apprentice that he will cause him to be instructed to read and write and at the expiration of the said term. Give the said apprintice one new Bible that the said apprentice shall not during the term aforesaid be Chargeable to the sd Town of Woodstock & at the end of sd term will deliver to the sd apprentice Double apparel of ordinary dress one suite of which to be new.

Occasionally all was not smooth sailing during the "said term" of these apprentices, and that the town kept a sort of guardianship over them is shown by two dissolutions of apprenticeships noted in the records; one of

William H. to Isaac M. on account of the said Isaac's having "misused and evil treated him the said Apprentice in an unlawful manner by Knocking him down with his fist and kicking him after laying on the ground—and for not giving the said Apprentice sufficient victuals &c"; another that of a young girl to a farmer who "misused and evil treated her and…corrupted the Morals Destroyed the virtue and injured the character of sd apprentice." The farmer fled and could not be found.

Slaves helped the pioneers of Woodstock till their fields and accomplish the work of the house. We see from the records quoted by Sylvester that the Dumonts, the Bonesteels, the Riselers, Rowes, Longyears, etc. all owned slaves. In the year 1814, according to the census, there were eight slaves in the township. In the record at the town clerk's office may be seen the indenture of a black girl, Gin, born of a slave, who is bound out by the overseers of the poor in 1806 to Michael Smith of Woodstock to:

dwell and serve from this day and date until she the said Gin Shall accomplish the full age of twenty five years, during all which terme the said Gin her master faithfully shall serve on all lawful business according to her power wit and ability;…that he the said Michael Smith the said Gin in all things shall learn her or Cause her to be learnt to Read the bible well and properly and cause her to be taught instructed in all kind of housework and during all the term above mentioned provide and allow unto the said Gin competent and sufficient meat and drink and apperal washing lodging mending and all things fit for Such Servant girl…and will make allow and provide and deliver unto her the said Gin one good suit of holy day Cloth of the Value of twelf dollars and fifty cents and other Sufficient every day Clothes for Such Slave (at the end of the term).

CLOTHING AND OTHER GOODS

Speaking of clothes, Mrs. Washington Riseley remembers when Disch's mill, later a gristmill, was used to make cloth. Her father rented it from Livingston. Under the east end stood big dyeing cans, and at the west end was the machine to card wool. People would spin their wool and then take it to the mill to be dyed, shrunk and made into cloth. She remembers that the cloth for older people was usually dyed different shades of brown, but children's materials were colored bright red or striped. Mrs. Riseley says the girls used to weave white linen collars and cuffs from their own flax, which they wore with their dark dresses to singing school. At the same or somewhat later date, the farmers' shirts were of unbleached cotton with full sleeves and band cuffs, and particular wives washed these every day and laid them out on the grass to bleach. All clothes, men's, women's and children's, were made up in the home, often by traveling seamstresses who put in a week or so at each place.

You may be interested in hearing what household articles our pioneers had and what they cost. Following are some early bills of sale: In October 1808, Ebenezer Griffin sold to Philip Bonesteel for ten dollars "one blacksmith bellows, one anvil, one Sledge, two hand hammers, Six small pinchers, one large pincher, four pair of Blacksmith tongs and other Small tools. Also household, namely one Bed and Bedding, two Chests and half dozin Chairs, three waterpails, one pair of fire Irons, Shovel and tongs, frying pan, Griddle Spider, two pots, two or three Barrels, one churn, one Closet, one trammel, and all goods mentioned in the Schedule hereunto annexed." (You probably know that a trammel is a hook set in the back bar of the fireplace from which to hang a pot.)

On February 2, 1812, Henry Shultis sold to Philip Rick for fifty dollars "one brown Mare, four Chairs, Bed and Brding, one Chest at my Father's, one yoak of oxen, likewise all furniture."

In April 1818, Henry P. Harder, of Woodstock, sold to Hannah P. Harder of Clermont, for $141.05, "2 horses and a set of Harness, one Iron Shod, Sled, a Plough and a Sett of Iron Harrow teeth, one Cross Cut Saw and a Yoke of Oxen, and two Ox Chains, Two Cows, a Loom and all the Household furniture and all the Grain and Hay in the Barn & likewhie the Grain on the Field & a Lot of Flax."

At about the same time, Thaddeus Thompson of Woodstock sold to Thaddeus Thompson Jr. for $187.23 "one sorrel horse, one light bay mare, one desk, one brass kettle, one large iron kettle, one set of wagon harness, one Plough & seven silver teaspoons, one Feather bed and two bedsteads, one woman's saddle, one wagon, one Sleigh, one Brown."

Early Census

A census was taken in Woodstock during 1814 by Stephen De Forest. The result was recorded as follows:

Electors possessed of freeholds of the Value of 100 pounds, 73. Electors of freeholds of the Value of 20 and under 100 pounds, 42. Electors not possessed of freeholds but who Rent tenements of the yearly value of 40

Shillings, 61. Free white males of the age of 13 years and under 45 years, 51. Free white males of the age of 45 years and upwards, 2. Free white females under 14 years of age, 27. Free white females of the age of 13 years and under 45 years, 78. Free white females of the age of 45 years and up, 46. All other free persons, 69. Slaves, 8.

Some interesting facts are shown here. First, that the number of persons owning their own farms is nearly twice as many as the renters. The Livingstons, then, were not as exclusively owners of the farms as the Down Rent agitation, thirty years later, might lead one to suppose. Second, that the women of a (roughly speaking) marriageable age outnumbered the men about one and a half times; while of women over forty-five there were more than twenty times as many as men—forty-six to two. Apparently the women withstood best the hardships of pioneer life; or was it that the men drank more hard cider?

HISTORY AND HEARSAY—THE DOWN RENT WAR

By Anita Smith

Editor's Note: The following selection is taken from Anita Smith's "History and Hearsay" essay, which appeared in the July 1931 edition of the Publications of the Historical Society of Woodstock. *The Down Rent War was a response by tenants in upstate New York, including Woodstock, to the feudal-type leases that wealthy landowners imposed on area farmers. Unable to ever secure the lands for themselves, despite the number of years they worked and improved the property, farmers, often disguised as Indians, began to retaliate against the onerous and burdensome system imposed upon them by the Livingston family. Throughout this period of brief "rebellion," agents of the landlord often found their work interfered with and their lives threatened by the anti-renters.*

The anti-rent agitation does not appear to have grown serious in our county until about 1845. At least we know from accounts found by Mrs. Zimm in old files of the *Ulster Republican* that the excitement was intense enough then to cause Major General Smith in Kingston to appeal to the adjutant general in Albany for arms from the State Arsenal to equip the local authorities to quell the disturbance.

There are still many people living whose parents took part in this little rebellion. Cattle horns were blown through the hills to call the "Down Renters" together. There were torchlight parades along the old plank road; and to prevent recognition, the men disguised themselves completely. Calico Indians they were called, from the calico blouses they wore, which hung to

A horn used during the Down Rent uprising in Woodstock. Anti-renters would blow the horn when agents of the landlord or local law enforcement approached the area.

their knees. Over their heads sometimes were worn sheepskin hoods that covered their faces, and into which holes were cut for the eyes. Upon this covering were sewn feathers and horsehair decorations.

One of my neighbors remembers his father's description of an event that took place during the rebellion around Cooper's Lake. John Lasher, an agent for the Livingstons, had been given the property known as the Lake Farm, over which there had been some dispute. One March day he went there in the snow to draw out of the woods some logs felled by the tenants. As soon as he was observed from across the lake there sounded the penetrating blow of a cattle horn calling out the "Indians," who, before long, surrounded him as he worked on the mountainside. A scuffle followed, in which some of the men falling off a cliff lost their headdresses and were recognized. Lasher managed to run off as far as the shore of the lake before he was caught. Then the Indians turned to Peter Sangendorf's barns nearby and, finding some tar in a barrel, daubed it upon their victim and added chicken feathers from the henhouse alongside before they allowed the unfortunate Lasher to get away.

This tar and feathering incident caused great excitement and was referred to in the official reports submitted to the governor. A posse under a sheriff was dispatched to apprehend some of the participants. When two of the men were arrested, they were surrounded by a band of Indians and the prisoners rescued. Thereafter, many of the agitators were obliged to hide. Bill Diamond, who had been recognized by his boots while taking part in the attack on the sheriff, hid for six months in a cave in back of the Van de Bogarts' house. The story goes that Peter Sagendorf spent many days hidden in the swamp around the lake. Parties of Indians kept watch on Cooper's Hill for the tax collector or sheriff. Merritt Staples tells of his father, Ephram Staples, who carried food to the concealed men when he was a lad. He says it was his Uncle Elias who shot the cap off the sheriff's head near the Coopers' house.

Emotions were aroused to such a high pitch that everyone was obliged to show their opinions. Thus one day, as the Widow Carl was preparing breakfast for her three boys, a group of Indians passed her window shouting "Down Rent," to which she was expected to reply in kind. However, the lady seems to have been independent minded and retorted, "Up Rent!" Whereupon the Indians entered her house and, taking her batter jug, poured the contents in fanciful patterns all over her kitchen floor.

Joab Eighmey, living in Silver Hollow above Willow, was a great Down Renter and the authorities were after him. He had difficulty marketing his lumber and tanbark, and always took a boy along in his "bark-riggin" so if a sheriff was met he could jump off and hide, leaving the boy to drive on.

Eventually a posse was sent up to Joab's farm. Directing them was Zalmon Olmstead, whose brother, Josie, was among the Indians ambushed on the hill. The sheriff's party ran the Indians into a black ash swamp. From there, one of the Indians fired at the sheriff and hit the bone button of his coat, which fortunately saved his life.

Not all the community joined in these demonstrations, and some of the best citizens of that time disapproved of the lawlessness. Meetings were held in Willow, then known as Little Shandaken, of citizens in favor of supporting

Cooper Lake, where much of the Down Rent "uprising" took place in Woodstock. *Photo by Richard Heppner.*

the law. Among them were many persons friendly to the anti-renters. In the meantime, all over New York State interest had been aroused over the conditions of the proprietary leases. The anti-rent candidate, Governor Young, was elected to office. Under his administration, the legislature in Albany made laws favoring the tenant farmers and abolished leasing agricultural land for more than twelve years.

LETTERS FROM THE CIVIL WAR

From HSW Archives

*E*ditor's Note: As the nation plunged into Civil War in 1861, Woodstock was as remote from the center of the national storm as any town could be. While Woodstock had not been immune to the practice of slavery in its early history, the last slaves to work the farms or serve in domestic capacities were now but a part of tales told about village life fifty years earlier. At war's start, the primary concern of isolated Woodstockers centered not on emancipation or economic connections with the South, but on their own economy and on what living could be forged from the Catskill Mountain landscape. Still, as was the case with most towns and villages across the land, the war called the sons of Woodstock away from their farms, the mills and their families. And, as the letters that follow offer, patriotism and support for the war was not absent from the Woodstock character.

   Letters home are a part of all wars. When read with detachment and through the filter of time, they offer yet another record of a unique event in history. But for soldiers like Aaron Longyear, they become more than just a connection between their individual circumstance and family back home. They are, in fact, part confessional, part expression of relief and, more importantly, an affirmation of life at its most fundamental level. For in combat, only the lucky ones get to write letters home.

AARON LONGYEAR

Born in 1840, Aaron Longyear was the son of John and Nelly Longyear. Enlisting at the beginning of the war, he was a member of Company I, 120th Regiment. His sister, to whom the letters that follow are addressed, was Catherine Longyear, wife of Peter Risely. The "Delia" referred to in the letters was Catherine and Peter's daughter Adelia. John W. Davis, as mentioned by Longyear, was John Whitbeck Davis, also of Woodstock. Davis, who would live well into the 1930s, was Woodstock's oldest surviving Civil War veteran at the time of his death. The mention of General McDowell and General Hatch in the first letter indicates that Longyear was describing the aftermath—and the ill feelings among soldiers—that followed the second Battle of Bull Run.

Longyear was taken prisoner a short time after these letters were written. He spent the remainder of the war in Southern prisons, including Andersonville (as did Eugene Johnson, another Woodstock veteran of the war who is referenced in the letter below as "Johnson's son"). Ultimately, like so many soldiers, it would not be a musket ball that would end Longyear's life, but disease brought on by the harsh conditions of prison life. Aaron Longyear would die near Alexandria, Virginia, on January 14, 1865, just three months shy of war's end. Longyear's letters appeared in volume 14 of the *Publications of the Historical Society of Woodstock*, published in 1939. The letters appear exactly as written.

Virginia, Sept. 18th, 1862.

Dear Sister:

I received your most welcome letter two evenings ago and will now answer. I would have answer befor but I was taken the same night that I received your letter with the tooth ache the next morning my face was swollen up at a tremendous rate. I looked as though I had been bitten by a Southern Gal and the poison from her teeth had taken effect For they are poison to the Government and must be also to the skin. It is some better now and will be all right in a day or so. We have moved twice since I wrote you last. The first time about twenty miles we were then the farthest advanced of all the Regiments in that direction We staid there about five days then moved to the place we are now about a mile from Alexandria. We are again under marching orders ready to start at a moments notice for the battle front in Maryland We may be called on at any moment perhaps now while I am writing the message is comeing I say let it come and we will do all we can to protect the stars and stripes and if we fall we have the consolation of doing our duty—all we ask for those at Home is their prayers for our success and I think God will crown us with success and our enemies fly before us in confusion—last Sunday there was a great battle in Maryland a very severe one too around Harpers Ferry that place was evacuated by the Rebels. They retreated and left us in command of the field We have taken a number of prisoners. General McClellan is still in pursuit of them We again begin to hope I think now there will be something done and the Stars & Stripes [will fly] again over those place which have been lately taken by the Rebels You wished to know something about the twentieth, I have seen a number of them They laid just a short distance from us after their hard fight but now they are gone again to the Battle field except a few who were unable to go. James Bonesteel's Son was in our camp Tuesday He staid all night with us. There is about three Hundred and fifty of them left including Horslers men who take care of the sick & all They were cut up very badly and they all say it was through General McDowell who they consider a traitor and they say if he had a showed himself in front every musket would fired at him. General Hatch who is under McDowell gave them the order to retreat. He took the responsibility on himself if you could hear them tell how they have been put through you would think it ruff

The Major of our Regiment arrived Tuesday He was Captain in the 20th and was wounded in the head but is all right now You know him his name is Tappen he was in the store with his brother in Kingston before he whent to the war. He is a very fine fellow and a noble officer. The Regiment is proud of him We have a few rather poor Officers in our Regiment but I am in hopes that they will soon learn more. John W Davis is well He received a letter from Home the same even'g that I received yours I have postage stamps enough for the preasent I bought a Dollars worth the other day I came across them I will let you know when I wish them I thank you for those you did send I will now close Please write soon My love to all the Family Kiss Delia for me and tell her to be a nice Girl

Ever your Brother
Aaron Longyear

Just as I finished my letter who should I see comeing but Johnsons son from Bristol He looks well and Healthy he is escaped all right He said he had written Home since the last Battle He was in He is in our camp now talking to the Woodstock Boys

Your brother A.L.

Gravestone of Civil War veteran buried in Woodstock Cemetery. *Photo by Richard Heppner.*

Letters from the Civil War

Dear Sister Brother Nieces

All

   I received your letter a number of days ago and I will now answer I received your letter before the battle at Fredericksburg in which we took part On the morning of the opening of the battle we were ordered to prepare to move We arose at 12 oclock at night had rating given out and at sunrise we started we had only two miles to go We marched to the banks of the Rappahannock where we halted We could see the whole of the fight We laid on a Hill right opposite the City The third day we were ordered to cross Rap-River and proceed in front We done so in double quick time, when we arrived on the field of battle the first thing we knew was to fall down on the ground to give room for the balls to pass over our heads. We were then but a short distance from the enemies line of battle. We sent skirmishes out. Fireing was kept up all night by them as soon as any of us arose to look around the balls would come at our heads. We had to lay low We you will understand occupied the center of the fight. The day before we arrived our men had drove the rebs in the woods with great slaughter on both sides They were carrying the dead off when we arrived & wounded The groans of the wounded and noise of the cannon made you think that you was in the midst of the fight. No one but those who have been there can have the least idea of a battle Well we laid here for two nights & days then we whent in the rear and formed the second line of battle & that very night we retreated back across the River everything was done with coolness. It was a grand retreat. Our regiment took it very cool and but one of our men was wounded It was very lucky for us. The Rebs had Batteries planted all through the woods and if we had attempted to charge in the woods we would have been all cut up. We are not in winter quarters yet We moved yesterday where there is plenty of wood and some think we will winter here but I doubt it A great many of the Regiment has been sick since the battle I am very well except a cold. Beck stands it good. We cannot tell when the war will end The boys will all be married by the time I come back. Well all right I will stand a better sight When you write you can send me a few postage stamps for we cannot buy them here. I am sorry to hear that John has broke his wagon. It is Sunday today but like any other day to us. Please give my love to all enquiring Friends and excuse bad writeing for I write this with paper on my knee

From your Brother
A Longyear.

Overlook Winters

By Jean White

Editor's Note: On a spring day in 1950, Sarah MacDaniel Cashdollar sat down with her daughters and grandchildren in the family parlor and recalled experiences from her life as a child on Overlook Mountain and, later, as a young wife and mother as she and her husband Wilbur served as caretakers of the Overlook Mountain House. The following stories, as recalled by her granddaughter, offer a firsthand account of winters on Overlook Mountain.

Standing guard like a protective mother, Overlook Mountain hovers over the little village of Woodstock. All of my life I have heard Overlook discussed with reverence and affection for its sheltering presence, its life giving nature and its serene beauty. My immediate ancestors began their lives there on "The Plains," cutting wood for the glass factories on the mountain and down in Bristol [Shady], farming acres on Overlook and Indian Head and later providing a comfortable place to stay for travelers and visitors through operating boardinghouses on the mountain and in the village. There were strong women then who lovingly tended and ministered to their families and homes, but whose help was also important in cutting wood, shaving shingles, harvesting hay and helping with nearly all of the farm chores. The following is about one of those women, Sarah MacDaniel Cashdollar, my grandmother, and is told in her voice.

One day in the winter of 1888, a whole sleigh full of young folks came down from the mountain to a donation at the Methodist Hall. It looked like snow was coming, but we didn't think much about it. We got to the hall around 7:00 or 8:00 p.m. and when we came out around 1:00 a.m. the snow was coming down in sheets! It measured about eight inches then and everyone asked, "How WILL we get home?" Well, my friend Jenny said, "Sarah, why don't you stay with me tonight?" She was working for old Dr. Smith. His place was near Larry Elwyn's corner, so I went and stayed with her. Well, I stayed for a week! Dr. Smith used to tease me that I'd have a board bill to pay. I had to stay until Barney could come and get me. Of course they had to shovel out at home first. When he came with horse and sleigh, we had to go through the fields right over stone walls on top of the snow. The farmers had made the stone walls; there were so many of them. You don't see them much anymore.

When we finally did reach home, all I could see in the front of the house were the upstairs windows! "For mercy sake," I said to Barney, "what's that?" He said that the snow had drifted up against the house and the whole first floor was covered. We drove around the back to get to the kitchen door. The boys had shoveled a tunnel right through the snowdrifts to reach the entrance. When we got inside the house, they started to tell me what fun they had shoveling in. Lincoln said, "We went upstairs and opened a window and Granville [Reynolds] went out [Granville was working there at the time]. He was going to start shoveling in toward the kitchen but because the snow was so loose close to the house Granville sank right down to the window in the kitchen. We had to go down and open the window to take him in!" Lincoln continued, "Now, we'll have to try it over again." We went upstairs and took mother's ironing board. We put it out through the second-story window and slid down on it right on top of the drifted snow. Then we were able to dig back to the kitchen door.

There was a deep brook by the apple orchard that Father had planted and the snow had just filled the brook and covered the trees so that only the top branches were in sight. When the snow was hard and crusty, we children went out the upstairs windows, walked across on the crust and tied white rags to the branches of the apple trees. When spring came and the snow cleared, the brook began to run again and you could see those white rags waving in the treetops. When folks saw them, they asked how they got there. We told them, "We tied them on." When they asked, "How did you do that?" we told them that we walked!

[Ten years after the Blizzard of '88, Sarah again encountered another storm on Overlook as she and her husband Wilbur worked as caretakers of the Overlook Mountain House.]

Overlook Winters

During the winter of 1898, we had one of the worst storms! The wind blew the smokestack and the large chimney down from the hotel. It took the engine house door (it ran on tracks inside the engine house) and threw it against the cottage. Then came a two-by-four over from the hotel, struck the bottom of a window in the cottage and broke the whole window out. Wilbur said, "What will we do?" I had the presence of mind to run upstairs and get a bed mattress off one of the single beds and brought that down and slapped it across the window. We nailed slats across it to keep it in place. Just when we got it nailed shut, another window upstairs went. Madlin had a little set of dishes she had been sent for Christmas on a stand under the window. The wind did the very same thing there. We took another mattress and slats and fixed that one as well. Then, the next thing, a chimney in the cottage started to blow off. First one chimney went and then the other one went. It was a bright moonlit night, the moon was shining bright. I got another mattress and brought the children down in the living room. As we lay there, we saw what we thought were clouds going overhead. Looking closer, what we saw were two-by-fours, whole sections of the hotel porch, roof and floor panels flying above us. Some pieces were fourteen feet square and blew over the cottage and landed in the trees. The wind kept up all night.

In the morning, Wilbur wanted to go check on the horses in the barn. He wrapped an old blanket around his shoulders and went out. The wind was blowing so hard that the barn roof was flapping up and down, up and down. It had pulled loose from the edge. Well, he got some steel spikes and drove one into the roof. He held onto that one and then drove another in until the roof looked like it was going to stay. While he was down there, I was in the house with the children. We had one man working there, John Twooten. Since Wilbur was gone so long, I tried to get John to go check on him. He wouldn't go. He just sat there with his boots and mittens on, but he wouldn't go out. So I said that I'd go. John said, "Don't make a fool of yourself. You can't go out there." Well, experience is my best teacher, so I got ready and started out. When I got outside, I didn't get very far and the wind blew me right back against the cottage. I crawled back into the house on my hands and knees. I no sooner got in then the children called from upstairs, "Mother, the house is on fire!" I rushed upstairs to see what was the matter. Flames were coming into the room through a hole in the chimney. Once there must have been a stovepipe connected to the chimney for that room. You could see that a large tomato can had been put in there to plug the hole. The fire in the chimney had melted it and the blaze was coming out into the bedroom. I called to John downstairs to get some cabbage leaves and put them in the stove. Using a pail of water and a ladle, I poured water through the hole in the chimney until the fire was out.

When I came downstairs, your father hadn't come back yet. Pretty soon I saw something coming over from the engine house like a cloud billowing. It looked like a parachute! There was a "thud" against the cottage. It was your father! As he was returning from the barn, he had come up the hill on his hands and knees clinging to the gravel, when the wind got under his blanket and took him up like a balloon! It blew him over the drifted snow and dropped him down by the house. We had to go around to the other side of the cottage and bring him in.

In the winter of 1899, we had a terrible ice storm. It rained and froze for three days. We couldn't get out and no one could come to us. We were like ships at sea. Walking was nearly impossible because the grass was all knobby with the ice. The ice on the guy wires from the hotel was so thick that pieces broke off because the wires couldn't hold the weight. We used a tape measure and found that the ice on the guy wires measured thirteen inches around and the ice collected on the telephone wires measured eight inches. There were three balsam trees in a cluster in front of the cottage that froze into a block of ice. It was as clear as crystal! You could look right through it and see the trees just as plain as could be. Many trees were bent and some split. But oh, the telephone! It never worked better! Sunday we entertained ourselves by taking down the telephone and calling Mother down home. They played the

Winter in Woodstock, Woodstock village under a fresh blanket of snow.

organ and sang hymns to us and we'd listen and then Wilbur would play his concertina and we'd sing back to them. (It was like having church anyway.)

When the ice began to break off, it was goodbye telephone! When the sun came out we went out to see if the way was cleared; honestly, it looked like a fairyland. Everything glittered just like diamonds. It was a beautiful sight. If we only had a camera in those days it would have been marvelous. When the ice started to release from the bushes, trees and wires, you heard it go down those mountain cliffs. Oh, it was like thousands of barrels of china. It went ting-a-ling, ting-a-ling, ting-a-ling and you heard that all the way down in the distance, you know. It was beautiful to look at, but it did a lot of damage too. Trees split and limbs broke off. Ice got into the gutters of the hotel and your father had an awful job getting the gutters opened up.

I often think of those days. We had good times and some hard times. We made our own fun, since we were quite isolated up there. Having large families made it easy to have parties. Sometimes we'd have a party with our own family. You needed to see the humor in things when so much time was devoted to hard work. I think we enjoyed ourselves and the good times because of the rather difficult tasks in just the day-to-day living.

EARLY DAYS AT WOODSTOCK

By Bolton Brown

Editor's Note: The following essay, written by Bolton Brown, was published by the Historical Society in 1933. Along with Hervey White (who would later go on to found the Maverick Art Colony), Bolton Brown was hired by Ralph Whitehead to seek a location suitable to match Whitehead's vision of an art colony. It was in that pursuit that Brown's arrival in Woodstock on a spring day in 1902 would dramatically shift the course of Woodstock history. Here Brown, founder of the Stanford University art department and a renowned lithographer and painter, recounts the events that led to the establishment of the Byrdcliffe Art Colony in Woodstock.

On the grounds that I was there from the beginning, I have been asked to write something about the early days at Woodstock. I am glad to do this, but here give notice that I shall not write as a historian and comprehensively, with dates and confirmations; I shall write simply some personal memories that come to me when I think of those times.

It is true that I was there before the colony was; in fact, it was I who brought the colony to Woodstock. The primary idea of the thing, however, came from Whitehead, who also furnished the money. He would be the natural one to write this article, but since he has been dead some years, and since Hervey White declined when I put it to him, I will myself, as I have said, set down a few memories.

Ralph Radcliffe Whitehead was an English gentleman, graduate of Oxford and friend of Wm. Morris and Ruskin, the ideas of whom influenced

Ralph Whitehead (left), founder of the Byrdcliffe Art Colony. Also pictured are Hervey White (center), who would later establish the Maverick Art Colony, and Fritz van der Loo (right).

him. He inherited a water faucet that flowed money whenever he turned it on. He lived in Santa Barbara and his age, when he comes into this tale, was fifty-two. His wife was from an old Philadelphia family and they had two young sons. Whitehead was small rather than large, thin rather than fat, had a nervous temperament and an amiable social manner. The impulse to establish a colony of artists had been with him for many years. As he thought of it, it seemed as if he would like to live there. "Artists," he once remarked, "are the only people in the world worth living with, and the most difficult."

I had a home in Palo Alto, and functioned as a professor at Stanford University. One day, thirty years ago, a gentleman appeared in our sitting room, stranger to me, but who presently became this man Whitehead. Art in general and art in particular we discussed and in the end there emerged this colony notion. When we had sounded each other out and come down to cases, he revealed that it was his desire to try to put this idea into effect, somewhere in the East, and offered me a salary to help get it going. His first figure I declined, as also his double of it; but when he tripled it, I accepted. Ours was purely a gentlemen's agreement; no papers were drawn. Time and money were verbally agreed upon and our general objective, that was all.

The question to be considered first was, where might we best locate; and Whitehead, thinking of a personal residence, laid it down that we must be in the country and at least fifteen hundred feet above sea level. "And I won't go to the Catskills," he declared, "they are full of Jews." He gave his vote for Asheville, North Carolina, which I rejected with energy, laying it down in my turn that we must be near the center of population and civilization—in a word, near the great cities in the northeastern corner of the United States. I pointed out that of these cities, New York was to be preferred and that the only land fifteen hundred feet high near this town was the Catskills.

Hervey White was a young man in those days—very much the poet—long hair, whiskers, no hat, red necktie and strong for radicalism in every form. The underdog was always right, with Hervey. He graduated from Harvard, but is far prouder of hailing from a ranch in Kansas. Whitehead, being fond of Hervey, made him a guest and sort of companion. So Whitehead said, "All right. Hervey and I will go south and see what we can find and you go north and see what you can find. We will keep in touch and decide about our location later." Exactly so. I sold my Palo Alto property, boxed my stuff and took the wife and three babies on the overland train for the East. I remember that after we had left Buffalo and were roaring through the forests east of it, out of the car windows we saw the floor of the woods sparkling with the yellow blossoms of adder's tongue. This was in the spring of 1902.

My ancestral home is up in Schuyler County. To it I now took my family and there left them. I went down to the town of Catskill. I provided myself with the government Geological Survey maps of the entire region that includes the Catskill Mountains. A stage took me up the northern side of the range to Windham. To describe my operations from this point would require a book, not an article. Sometimes I traveled by horse and buggy, but quite as often on my feet. Much of the country I explored was without roads or even paths, and it was by virtue of my contour maps that I was able to go, afoot and alone, over the highest ridges and mountains in the group. I scrambled over summits so wild it seemed no man or even animal could ever have been there. Some were flat table rock, covered everywhere with dry, gray, dead moss a foot thick, the same gray moss hanging in sad festoons from all the branches of the few stunted spruce trees that barely survived. I am an old hand at mountain work, having served my apprenticeship in the wildest of the California Sierra, but for sheer savage impenetrability and utter laboriousness some of these Catskill trips really capped my experience. I tore and ripped my clothes, on one occasion, to an extent that forced me, on regaining the region of farms, to borrow a threaded needle and retire with it round the corner of the house and sew myself up before I could meet people.

As the crow flies, the Catskills are only some twenty-five miles across, but I used up three entirely laborious weeks zigzagging back and forth and plunging up and down in them. I got in a high pocket with steep walls, in its bottom a single minute farm. The man said the name of the place was Mink Hollow. South of this hollow, the map showed that the steep wall terminated in a narrow and high ridge. Still south of this spruce-crested ridge, across a valley, the map gave Mount Overlook—a lake appearing off to the east. Lakes being scarce and desirable, I scrambled some miles down to this one, only to find it no lake at all but merely one of the Kingston reservoirs—named, however, Cooper's Lake. The day being still young, I walked up the backside of Overlook, emerging into the notch at Mead's Mountain House.

Exactly here the story of modern Woodstock really begins, for it was just at this moment and from this place that I, like Balboa from his "peak in Darien," first saw my South Sea. South indeed it was and wide and almost as blue as the sea, that extraordinarily beautiful view, amazing in extent, the silver Hudson losing itself in remote haze, those farthest and faintest humps along the horizon being the Shawangunk Mountains. I walked slowly along the highway facing this panorama, passed by the porch of the Mountain House, and a little down the road came upon an old man with a white beard doing something over in an apple orchard—all the trees in

Located on Overlook Mountain, the Mead's Mountain House served as one of Woodstock's primary boardinghouses for summer visitors. It was near this site, in 1902, that Bolton Brown first observed the village of Woodstock.

full blossom. I climbed the stone wall and talked with him. He registered surprise and disapprobation at my coming "alone" over those mountains back of Mink Hollow. It was very dangerous, he said. He did not know that he was talking to a chap who had climbed Mount Shasta, "alone." I was rude to his mountains, I confess, for I said, "These are the littlest mountains I have ever seen."

My old man was Mr. Mead himself, who had built the place forty years before. Pointing down to what seemed an earthly paradise, stretched at our feet, I asked, "What is the name of that place down there?" He replied, "That is Woodstock Village." It looked good to me then; it has not ceased to do so.

That afternoon I walked along the road past the blossoming orchard and down as far as the Snyder homestead (now Camelot). Having got below the forest belt and into the backfields, I traveled across lots, west, right over the territory now known as Byrdcliffe. It was cultivated fields then, and nothing else, barring some cows and gray nubs of rock sprinkled everywhere.

When I had made a few inquiries as to real estate values, I decided that this was the place for Whitehead's experiment. I wired him and we rigged a date in the city of Washington. We met and I recall that we talked about the fourth dimension and ate a planked steak for dinner. Upon my report of findings, Whitehead agreed that Hervey and he and I should go up and have a look. We arrived at Kingston and a livery took us through Woodstock and up to Mead's. After lunch, the three of us walked down to Snyder's and then west, just as I had previously done, as far as the region where the Whitehead residence now stands. We advanced in a wandering sort of way, looking around a good deal and conversing about the tract we were passing over. On the way back, we came to one of those sightly spots from which all the world was visible, and there sat down on the grass to talk and rest. Whitehead asked me whether I would absolutely refuse to go south for our enterprise. I gave an evasive answer, but stressed my strong belief that the north was the better place. We sat a while, pulling spears of grass, gazing at the view and making desultory remarks back and forth.

Finally Whitehead said, "Well, all right; let's have it here. We'll buy this row of farms along this side of the mountain," and he began to look both ways to see about how much that would be. He pointed to the home buildings of the different farms, commenting on their external appearance as an index to their value. None appeared particularly formidable until we came to consider the Riseley establishment (now the Lark's Nest). This looked serious and had large, good barns, painted red, and well-kept fields. "That fellow," said Whitehead, "will make trouble for us. He's got a good place and he'll want a big price for it."

Half in fun, we began to point out to each other where we would like to build. And Whitehead indicated, then and there, and named it White Pines, the spot where his house was subsequently built. When our legs grew cramped from long sitting on the ground, we rose, stretched ourselves and began to stroll back toward Mead's. "Very well, then that's settled," said our leader. "And I'll get right out of here back to California. I'll take the train tonight. If one of these farmers sees an Englishman in white flannels walking over his backfields, his price will be double in the morning. I will put ten thousand dollars in the Kingston Bank to your credit, Mr. Brown, and leave you to do the buying. You'll have to get options on all, you know, first. You can deal with these people: you know how: you are one of them; I'm a stranger—a foreigner, almost, I couldn't do it. Keep in touch with me and when your options are all in I'll have Gilman, my lawyer in New York, come up and close the matter."

The territory selected embraced six or seven different holdings and amounted in the total to perhaps twelve hundred acres. And just as I could not detail my three weeks of exploration, no more can I detail the months

White Pines, the Byrdcliffe home of Ralph Whitehead and his wife, Jane Byrd McCall Whitehead. *Photo by Richard Heppner.*

of experiences when I was left alone to wangle these farms out of the hands of their owners, men and women whose ancestral homes they were, whose living came out of these acres and who had no remotest notion of wanting to sell, or of why I wanted to buy.

Naturally, the first man I approached was eaten up with curiosity as to this last point, and until he got that straight he would not talk selling at all. Our projects being what they were, it was out of the question even to try to make any of these people understand the simple truth. It was a form of truth they had never come in contact with. And no matter what vague generalizations I coined for the occasion, my hearer always took it for granted that there was a nigger in the fence, who would jump out and make him sorry later if he didn't watch out. And the second man was just the same—in fact, they were all the same, in that matter. They went backward, up, down and sideways, but never forward to meet my proposition. Between times they got to each other and evolved theories about me—I wanted to "start a park," or gold had been discovered, or I had a big hotel up my sleeve. During the evenings, Ed Harder's store was a rally of farmers, telling each other.

53

When a month had gone by and nothing had been accomplished that you could see with the naked eye, I decided to leave them a while, stewing in their own juice. I hinted that they had shown themselves a hopeless lot and that I was abandoning them. I went up and visited my family in Schuyler County, but I had a spy in Woodstock, nevertheless. When it seemed well to do so, I returned and started in over again.

The Snyder place, I learned, was held under a heavy mortgage by a Saugerties man named Otis, and it was long overdue and not even interest paid. Some family affair, it was; and the Snyders never expected to be asked for any money. But when I approached Otis he at once offered to sell for the face of the mortgage. I scrawled an option and he signed it.

Next to the Snyder land, on the west, lay the farm of one Fred Kelley, a younger man and a thorough rustic. No, he did not want to sell, nor even to talk about it. I could talk about it, as long as I pleased, but he had nothing whatever to say. I explained to him, I put arguments before him, I lectured at him, I muttered ominously, I sang seductively. I offered to take him out in a wagon and let him pick out a new farm and I would buy it and give it to him. Nothing doing. And at that the Kelley land was so bad you could hardly call it land at all—mostly cliffs, swamps and big stones. One day he was plowing, I trailing back and forth at his heels. At the end of the furrow, the horses rested and I pointed out to Fred the tons and tons of stone he turned over each year to no good at all. He did not even grin—just punched the tobacco tighter in his pipe and remarked, "I don't seem to mind it."

I gave him up—for that time. But later on in the season I found him swinging a scythe, trimming out the angles in the rail fence where the machine could not reach. Driving my buggy right into his field, I opened its seat and took out a small drawing board, a pen, a bottle of ink and a sheet of paper so inscribed that it only required Fred's signature to be a "legal option." Laying the paper enticingly on the board, I uncorked the ink, and, without words, took up my position just out of reach of my man's active elbow; and there I stayed while, equally silent, he ignored me and mowed rod after rod of fence corners. There was a tension about it, however, and at last, still wordless, Fred swung round, signed and went on mowing.

As Whitehead had predicted, I had trouble at the Riseley place, the one with the impressive barns. They, father and son, were hung off until the last and said one night that they would give an option for three thousand, but when I came the next morning to get it they demanded six. Since they were the last and the property was important to us, I took it.

Gilman, up from New York, smiled a little at the bunch of homemade options I handed him, but he admitted they were clear and would hold in any court of law. We went round and gave the owners notice to prepare deeds, for we were buying them all out. Mr. Snyder was in the road before his house when, on this ungracious errand, I walked up. I informed the old gentleman that Otis had sold his home to us. No reply at all did he give; he hardly saw me, after I had spoken, but just looked off beyond the river to the hills. And, feeling very mean, I turned away and left him standing there, tears running down his old bronzed cheeks.

Then there was John Rivenberg and his old wife. John was seventy-five, a veteran of the Civil War. An expert axe-man, he saw four years of fighting and never fired a gun—he just had to wade into streams and build bridges while sharpshooters practiced at his head. He was small, but tough and straight, even when I knew him. "Oh he was an iron-sided man!" said Levi Harder, his next-door neighbor. John and I foregathered under an apple tree in his orchard. We sat in the grass and talked and he told in detail how, field after field and year by year, he had gradually secured the land of his hundred-acre farm. It was a beautiful story. And if you did not hear it, it was not John's fault, for when he talked he shouted. He would walk twelve miles to do an errand in Kingston sooner than pay railroad fare. "I'm seventy-five now. I'm livin' on borrowed time," he said. "No, I ain't got a tooth in my head; ain't had for twenty years," says he. "Why John, what do you chew with?" "With me gooms." He expressed a willingness to sell. "Oh yas, I'll sell," he bawled, "but the woman she won't sign off." "It's my home," was what the woman said.

When the buying was finished and the fall was threatening to pass into winter, Whitehead came on again from the west. Hervey reappeared from somewhere, bringing along as a chum one Fritz van der Loo, ex-cavalry captain under De Wet in the Boer war. He showed me a scar on his breast and another on his back where an English lancer stuck a spear through him. He was a jovial party, fond of cooking and used to get up wonderful dinners. Now he lives in China. Carl Lindin, painter, dropped from somewhere—I think it was Chicago. Lindin originated as a boy on his father's farm in Sweden. Aside from painting, his specialty seemed to be making a hit with the ladies. In those days, the house in which he now lives, on a rock ledge above the road, was a disused church. Hervey and Lindin camped in it for a while. One evening the three of us were sitting there, by the stove, when Cashdollar came in. He had a bushel of chestnuts to sell, and offered them to Hervey with the remark, "They're three dollars now, but if you want me to I'll hold them for you till they go down to a dollar and a half."

We rented one of Cal Short's barns, up at Rock City, boxed off a section, put in a window, a stovepipe hold and a stove and there we had

Barns along Rock City Road—on the way to Overlook Mountain—were favorite "rental" opportunities for artists arriving in Woodstock.

the first "studio" in Woodstock. Installed at a draughtsman's table I, jack of all trades, was transformed from a go-getter to an architect. I planned Whitehead a house and one for me. When built, he called his White Pines and mine is now Carniola. We decided other building sites—that of the library and dance hall, the eating house, a studio or two, a barn and so on—and, vaguely, the layout of roads to serve them. Whitehead put more money in the Kingston bank to my credit and disappeared into California for the winter. I got out and hired every able-bodied man I could see. One gang, with teams and lumber wagons, I sent out over the fields to gather up stones and haul them to where the pick and shovel men were sinking cellars and foundation trenches. Others ran pipes from springs up on the mountainside, in ditches three feet deep, sometimes through solid rock. A box-like shelter for the timekeeper was the first new building. A cold rain threatened and the men were for knocking off. My nimble riding pony carried me swiftly to Ed Harder's store, and before the rain had time to get going I was distributing to my workers free, oilcloth suits. Winter was coming; I could not afford to lose an hour.

Volunteers to lay up cellar walls were called for and promptly stepped up. "We're masons," they said. And while they laid walls and the wagons brought stones to them, I peeked through a little instrument and staked out the exact line of the roads—none having a grade greater than three degrees. And the road gang began to build roads. Lumber we would need and I roamed widely, searching out all the little local sawmills and buying, in more than one case, their entire stock. Some of the buildings called for unusually large beams. The mill man and I would go together into the woods to hunt out and mark, one by one, the chestnut and oak trees that would yield the beams we wanted. Fritz and Hervey, all this time, were also building themselves a house, over to the west, with their own gangs. They lived in it when it was done.

Carniola was designed for my family. Thirteen rooms opened off a central hall or gallery lighted by a skylight. The front door was eight feet wide and commanded all creation. The back door, opposite and across the hall, had the same width and opened so close to the mountain that we had to put steps from it up into the forest. Catamounts could come right into the house if they wanted to. One did. It got down into the cellar and hid. I saw its round head, back beyond a beam, its two eyes glaring from the light I held. The carpenters left their work to come and look and to evolve schemes for his destruction. But I was less hungry for blood than I was to get my house built, so I sent them back to their saws and nails and I suppose the catamount crept out that night and ran away.

Larry Plass was head carpenter at the group of buildings that centered on the library, while Charley Waters held the same position at my house. By the time the roof was on and the walls were closed in, it was dead winter—the men continued working just the same. In the stream below Shady, I chose out some nice stones, brought down a heavy wagon and hauled them up. With my own hands, I laid them into the main sitting room fireplace. It took me a week. To keep the new cement from freezing, I ran a little fire. We had zero weather. I was boarding at Mrs. Ella Riseley's, at Rock City. After supper I mounted Billy, my saddle horse, and rode up through the snow to my house. I led him inside and stood him in a corner, head outward, where he could see me. I replenished the little fire and then stretched myself on a carpenter's bench and lay so all night, rising at intervals to put on more wood. And the pony's eyes would shine, from the firelight. At early dawn I rode back—the air so cold you could hardly breathe it—to eat for breakfast Mrs. Riseley's buckwheat pancakes. Thus for a week I beat Jack Frost.

With the spring, the buildings were about finished, and by the time the season warmed, Whitehead came on again, this time bringing his family and favorite riding mustang, Janet. I moved my wife and three infants into our house. Hervey and Fritz got into their new quarters. The dance hall and library gradually got finished, also the eating hall and two or three studios. The Riseley farmhouse was remodeled into the Lark's Nest. By the time early summer had come, the real estate phase of our adventure was drifting to the rear, and the architectural phase was giving place to the social phase. We had the plant; now for the people.

Whitehead's friends in the art world took an interest. Some of them came and looked us over. A few established themselves for the summer. Birge Harrison bought adjacent land and built an imposing residence. Lindin, with $400, bought his church and surrounding land. From Boston came to us a painter six and a half feet high, Herman Dudley Murphy. Then there was a Scotchman—the only one in the crowd who could draw—Cameron, I think. And the man from New Zealand, Ernest Chapman, known colloquially as "the Brass Pounder," who made perforated objects out of sheet metal. George William Eggers, fresh from Pratt Institute, was one of us; also Warren Wheelock, of the same institution. Wheelock rented one of our rooms, working as a carpenter to pay for it. Nobody had much money, except Whitehead, but the rest of us were full of schemes to make some. One or two carved and gilded picture frames as an industry. Miss Little wove rugs. So, by the way did my wife; for we had bought the loom of old Mrs. Lewis, of Rock City, and set it up in our house. From Hull House, in

Chicago, came Miss Starr, maker of beautiful bookbindings, and with her a youthful apprentice. Numbers of art students, whose names escape me, appeared on the scene.

We organized—call it that—a school. Three of us, Murphy, Cameron and I, were the teachers. A student simply picked out which teacher he preferred. The dance hall was used as a studio, its walls to stick things on. The Whiteheads combined the first name of Mrs. Whitehead, Byrd, and the last part of Radcliffe, so creating the word Byrdcliffe. They wanted a seal, using this name, and they offered a "prize," five dollars I think it was, for the "winning design." I got in bad by refusing to compete. One of the students was so impressed with himself that he would only paint behind a screen, lest anyone should see how he did it. In the nature of the case, we had them of all sorts. One of Whitehead's young geniuses declared that he was "painting for posterity." He used to make cannon-like echoes by slamming the side of a building with a board and yelling. He achieved a berth in the lunatic asylum, ultimately. And there was Professor Schutze, from Chicago University, and his wife, Eva, and Eva made marvelous things with a camera. And there was Mrs. Howe, from California, who wrote "pastels." And Charlotte Perkins Stetson, who wrote brilliant subversive ideas.

Three nights a week we had a community dance at the dance hall. The eating house tables filled up. Extra people were accommodated in extra ways. A number came to our house and Lucy, my wife, gave them table board. For a while, we sat down fourteen at the table. We had a good woman in the kitchen to cook and Lucy hired Verna Herrick, daughter of Whitehead's boss carpenter, to take care of the children. As most of our boarders were women, men naturally occurred also—after dinner, sitting around in the summer twilight. We rented a room to Edith Wherry, raised in China, daughter of a missionary. Edith could talk Chinese and when we would ask her to, she would say the Lord's Prayer for us in that language. She was a writer, supposedly; and Murphy fell in love with her. She fell in love with Lindin.

Two other Pratt Institute people appeared, Zulma Steele and Edna Walker, cronies. Fritz went off and brought back from South America a delightful creature, his wife. One Vivian Bevans, at the dances was considered one of our beauties. She was supposed to harbor a smoldering passion for making pottery. Hervey afterward married her. But it was Zulma Steele who was really our outstanding lady, both visually and in a quality we may call style. Whitehead built a cottage studio for "Steely and Walker," as we called them, among the pines above his place, and employed the pair officially as "designers." The Lark's Nest was full of larks—in fact, so full that the larks got on each other's nerves to such an extent that we used to call the place the "Wasp's Nest." Miss Starr worked away at her bookbinding, and very lovely it was. She was boarding at the eating house when one of the students kissed one of the serving girls, an impropriety she at once reported to Whitehead for action. But he only said, "This isn't Hull House."

Then our taking in so many lady boarders threatened to breed a false center of gravity, as it were. Whitehead was all for "democracy," in theory; but down in his British subconscious, class consciousness was an influential ghost of medieval social arrangements—in scales, with steps up and steps down, and a central court and so forth and so on. The idea implied something like a benign reign over gracious and grateful dependents. But in twentieth-century America, this ideal found no suitable atmosphere. So again I was in bad. We never quarreled, Whitehead and I; we "differed." And seemingly more and more. One thing was the work in the art school. His notion was that everybody should do as he damned please, at any rate that he should primarily have a good time. Of self-discipline, or any other, he showed little appreciation. Whereas I knew that results of value always presuppose training. His thought was a happy-go-lucky Bohemia; my thought had little to do with Bohemia but a lot to do with understanding your job and working at it. Art, to Whitehead was an amusement, and the artists amusing; he was the dilettante personified. Naturally we differed. And when he found in me a disposition to stand for my ideas, he said I "mistook my position."

Our contract allowed either of us to terminate it on giving a year's notice, and Whitehead now gave me such notice. The first man in, I now became the first man out. I said to him, "If I go out and buy land in the neighborhood, am I to meet with oppositions and unpleasantnesses from here?" He replied, "I don't know anybody that would not be glad to have you settle in the neighborhood." So I went a mile to the east and bought forty acres of land from Ella Riseley for $600. I built a house and we lived in it. Also a studio forty rods back in the woods, in which I painted for seven years.

Hervey and Fritz did not last long, but migrated two miles south to the other side of Ohio Mountain and bought the farm now known as the Maverick. Miss Little ultimately moved out and established her loom and dye pots off east of the village. The Steele and Walker combination moved westward and established itself independently as a pottery. Lindin married and remodeled his church into a home. The Art Students' League established its summer school at Woodstock, building for it a dormitory in Rock City and a studio down on the banks of the Sawkill. The girl that could speak Chinese went to Paris and wrote a novel. And so, gradually, artists and near-artists, oozing out of Byrdcliffe or drifting in from the world at large, set up all over the region their widely varying establishments. And thus it was that the art colony entirely outgrew the original idea—a chosen and selected group, inside a fence—and became instead a large, free public movement that has been growing steadily for thirty years and is likely to grow thirty more.

THE FIRST SUMMER IN BYRDCLIFFE, 1902–03

By Lucy Brown

Editor's Note: In this selection, originally published in the second volume of the Publications of the Historical Society of Woodstock, Lucy Brown, wife of Bolton Brown, gracefully recounts life during the first year at Byrdcliffe and the people— both locals and arriving artists—she met along the way.

The summer began in October, when Shute Shultis met the Browns at West Hurley with a covered conveyance (after consideration that seems the best word) drawn by two gray horses. It was pouring rain and the unknown hills were deep in wet, wet mist. (It was that way in 1902, though hard to believe in this year of the Lord 1930, for in July the clothes mildewed in the closets from excessive damp.) After the chilling drive, we were vaguely relieved when we finally drew up by the horse block at the rear entrance of Ella Riseley's white house below Rock City, on the Overlook Road. The small, anxious-eyed little figure that ran out to welcome us embraced us forthwith in her comfortable hospitality. We found, in the big warm kitchen, Ella Riseley, Eva Riseley, a little blonde youngster, Mr. Hamm (the farm superintendent), the shaggy dog and wonderful buckwheat cakes for breakfast. I think the dog is the only member left unchanged; at least he is still a "Rover"—for Mr. Hamm has been translated; Little Eva is now Mrs. George Burt; and even our faithful Ella has turned into Mrs. Ellsworth Myer.

Mr. Hamm, even in those "pre" days, had a genial secret whereby he turned the contents of a barrel of cider into something rich and strange, by

Most Woodstock visitors arrived in Woodstock by taking a train to West Hurley and, from there, traveling the final few miles by wagon to Woodstock, disembarking in front of Rose's store.

the subtle application of sugar, raisins and certain distillates. I stopped in once, at a later date, on my way to our house on the hill, and being thirsty and new to the wine of the country, took a proffered goblet, and, finding it a strangely refreshing drink, yielded to Mr. Hamm's invitation to another glass before I left. By the time I reached Rock City—we walked in those days—the landscape began to grow glamorous and I was fain to sit on a very hard boulder that I might restore solidity to my world. I sat there a long, long time.

Building at Byrdcliffe began almost immediately: White Pines for the Whiteheads; the "Farmhouse" for Hervey; and Casa Carniola, where we were to live. During these winter months of construction there were intermittent visits from Mr. Whitehead. In addition to our group at the Riseleys', Hervey White and Carl Linden took sanctuary in the picturesque old German Lutheran church in the pine grove, afterward purchased by Linden and transformed into his present home. I fancy both these men were good cooks, a not uncommon artistic asset; at any rate, I remember their joining us once for supper at the Riseleys' and gravely reflecting on the subject of "that soft American cake," and not taking any, though I had made some very good creamy thing to go with it. There must have been concealed about Linden remote foreign standards of which in those days I was innocent! I remember Fritz van der Loo alarming me very much once by looking serious and saying, "But you can't give a man like Linden vegetables cooked in WATER!"

While we awaited the completion of the first Byrdcliffe houses, I made the acquaintance of old Mrs. Dubois, who had lived for years in the gray corner house opposite Rose McGee's. Mrs. Levi Harder tells me that in the days of the Glasco Turnpike that house was a milliner's shop! Mrs. Dubois (she was not one whom you would call by her first name) wove the residual rag of the countryside into strips of gay carpet, good, but just, battering it out on her great and ancient hand-hewn loom. A tall rawboned figure, with intelligent and powerful visage—it wasn't just a "face"—of prodigious memory and trenchant tongue, it is one of my life's regrets that I did not then and there take down some metres of her salty reminiscences. Well over seventy-five, she was fairly fixed as to habits and I remember that she couldn't or wouldn't eat a particle of fat, and sometimes displayed to me, in a shining pan under a snowy covering, strangely shredded bits of beef, designed for her meal, from which she had minutely dissected every suspicion of fatness. She, her house, her ancient frosted husband, who "carried" everything that was carried between Woodstock and West Hurley, all these affairs were clean, with a radiant idealism that simply awestruck me. Mrs. Dubois remains with me to this day as the epitome of all the fundamental virtues.

This being notably an "Arts and Crafts" world where we were to do—and simply—things with our hands, I developed a desire to make some ruggish weavings too, and being for those first months within a few moments' walk of Rock City, I went every day to my friend, and under her direction, when more important jobs were off the Dubois schedule, beat out for myself a gay and mongrel little rug. It was then about Christmastime, and in an attack of innocent gaiety, I dispatched the fruit of our loom to Mrs. Whitehead, who was then in the South, wrapping with it a box of self-made chocolates. In the charming acknowledgement, which ultimately I received, there was a delicate stressing of a possible future for me as a confectioner and—enough said. Fate has taken care to eliminate me as a menace.

In February, we went up to our house in Byrdcliffe; Mr. and Mrs. Whitehead came on from California in the early spring to their new home; Linden moved into studio quarters in the Lark's Nest group, while Hervey and Fritz took possession of the "Farmhouse."

Fritz van der Loo was one of those purely fictional characters who now and then occur in real life, and since I have often been asked by the newcomers as to who and what was Fritz van der Loo, I may say here that he was born and

Gathered before the fireplace in Byrdcliffe's Lark's Nest are (left to right) Ned Thatcher, Isabella Moore, Lucy Brown, Carl Eric Lindin, Ethel Canby, Byrdcliffe head cabinetmaker Erlensen, a woman who is unidentified and the woodcarver, Olaf Westerling.

brought up on a coffee plantation in Java, appeared in Africa at the time of the Boer war, became captain of de Wet's scouts and later met Hervey on board ship during an Atlantic crossing. Becoming friends, they later joined Mr. Whitehead in France and had some travel together. Fritz carried a tradition of vast coffee plantations and great family wealth in Paramaribo, whither Mr. Whitehead, with his customary generosity, sent him, some months later, to accumulate the ancestral treasure—if any. Unfortunately, the treasure was not forthcoming, but the yellow fever was, and Fritz ended by returning to America with the potential riches of a betrothal to a charming young woman of Dutch Guiana who later came to New York, where she was met, married and brought back in triumph to Byrdcliffe by her husband. Hervey forthwith gave over the occupancy of the Farmhouse to Fritz and Ella, while he himself floated between the Lark's Nest and a cabin of his own. Hervey's subsequent career as one of the makers of Woodstock history is too familiar to need recalling here; the best known and the best loved of all the colonists. (Applause.)

When summer came, Hervey and Linden took over the Lark's Nest cottages with the idea of developing there a group or club of super-interesting people who might ultimately draw more of the same. Hervey enlisted a Chicago friend of his by the name of Elizabeth Kryscher to superintend the dining room affairs of the house for this sophisticated set. I remember his saying at the time with his optimistic detachment, "Elizabeth is a charming woman! We are not asking of her anything but just to see that plates are hot, salads cold and meats rare." After wrestling with the situation—and most inadequate rustic help—through the season, I was not surprised to learn that Elizabeth had fled back to Chicago in the fall and married a widower with six; which I don't doubt she found extremely simple.

So far as I can remember, we counted the following that summer in the Lark's Nest cottages and on the hill who were to make or mark history: Charlotte Stetson Perkins Gilman of *The Cookstove and Eohippus* fame, and an acolyte of hers, by name Harriette Howe, who wrote *Pastels*, and who confided in me that the reason she had left her husband some years before in California was because shortly after they were married, on being asked if he would have some of the stewed blueberries, he replied, "Why yes, I'll take the juice." This claim indicated to his wife a depth of selfishness and Oedipus complexes (title then unknown) that to the suffering help meant nothing less than the divorce court, whither she presently hailed him.

Then there was Mary Manning, who wrote tales and ultimately turned into Mrs. Gosh; Olivia Dunbar, a lovely literary lady who, I think, became Mrs. Ridgeley Torrance; Mr. John Quincy Adams, of New York Civic Art Committee fame; and his wife, a notable housekeeper, who tried Miss Krysher somewhat as to the ethics of dishwashing; John Duncan, artist lithographer; Annette Butler, teacher of Sloyd from California; Mrs. Lou Wall Moore and daughter, both of whom danced professionally; Ellen Starr of Hull House, a famed binder of beautiful books; Martin Schutze from Chicago University, later to earn enduring fame as founder of the Woodstock Historical Society, and Eve Watson Schutze, his wife, both solid pillars for our construction. Among the younger set was George Eggers, art director today of one of New York's most important universities; Anderson, the illustrator; our Ned Thatcher; Westerling of the woodworkers; Ernest Chapman from New Zealand via Paris, painter and craftsman, who was dubbed the "brass beater."

On the hill, other houses were completed rapidly. Marie Little set up her looms in a strategic position between White Pines and a marvelous outlook over river, valley and distant ranges. Mr. and Mrs. Gino Perera moved into their spacious home not far from the Villetta, and one of the pleasures of those days most happily recalled was that of listening to Mr. Perera making music at the studio in the evening. It was almost a shock to realize that a

Chopin Nocturne could touch the depths of musical consciousness through the strings of a mandolin—but it did!

Then also came two young women from New York, popularly called "Steele and Walker." Zulma Steele, painter, potter, craftsman, is still one of the colony as Mrs. Nelson Parker, though Walker has left us for real life in Scotland. They built an attractive lodge on a green hill beyond White Pines and added greatly to our social riches.

Another figure who floats through that summer landscape for me is that of Edith Wherrey, a young friend who came to spend a fortnight with us and stayed all summer (they do that in Woodstock). Somebody called our Edith the "flamboyant bat," for when the dew fell and the stars began to twinkle over the hilltops she would wrap herself in a somber cape and flitter out, up and down the hill roads, joining the parties of nightriders, or walkers, doing Overlook, or haunting moonlit meadows and streams on the lookout for a pixie or so. Edith was much exhorted by Mrs. Charlotte Gilman as to her ways, but I doubt if it went very deep. Edith left Byrdcliffe in the fall with the poetess Florence Wilkinson for France; they avowing their intention to

Art students make their presence known on the streets of Woodstock, much to the chagrin of some locals.

open a salon in Paris—just like that! The next news I had of her was three years later, when we were living in our home on the Overlook Road. The letter from Paris said that she was to marry a young Canadian whom she wished to meet in the loveliest spot in the world and would I lend her the oak tree on our hinterland hill. So she arrived, homing straight from France to the Woodstock oak, stopping only to don a white gown and virginal green wreath before my mirror. One hour later a fair and warm young man appeared from Canada, who was, I thought, somewhat embarrassed by the stage setting. However, he washed his face and smoothed his hair (omitting the wreath) and disappeared in the direction of the oak tree. That was Edith. Afterward she wrote a successful book called *The Red Lantern*, a story of the Boxer rebellion, for she had been born and grew up in China; that may have accounted for her.

Meanwhile, students arrived, and there were Herman Dudley Murphy of Boston, Dawson Watson (then living in Camelot), Bolton Brown (then known as painter, but since of artist-lithography fame), for those who would paint and carve and be crafty day by day, and by night there was delightful opportunity in the studio (which somebody made the mistake of calling the "Casino") for dancing and playing around. Mr. and Mrs. Whitehead were interested in introducing us to some of the old country dances of England and elsewhere, and I think every one of us who shared them have treasured the memory of those delightful evenings. Denim and corduroy were the vogue in dress, and I think of the lamp-lit studio, the pre-jazz music and our quaint gyrations with vast pleasure.

Then, too, we were allowed the privilege of using the fine Whitehead library housed in the studio, and my memory holds from it many and beautiful books; we were on the fringes of the Mauve Decade and one could be and was, perhaps, unashamedly romantic. I read William Morris then, out of that library in the beautiful Kelmscott edition. Since then the world has turned over. Woodstock still offers us "library privileges," but now, instead of *The Well at the World's End* or *The Water of the Wondrous Isles* I read the three Sitwells, England's super sophistications. I leave with you one of Edith Sitwell's lovely lyrics:

> *Jane, Jane, as tall as a crane*
> *The morning light creaks down again.*
> *Comb your cockscomb ruffled hair;*
> *Jane, Jane, come down the stair.*

As the master detective in the English thriller says: "I wonder!"

THE MAVERICK

By Henry Morton Robinson

Editor's Note: Originally published in 1933, volume 11, Henry Morton Robinson's essay chronicles the creation of the Maverick Art Colony by Hervey White in 1905. White, who had been a part of Ralph Whitehead's efforts to establish the Byrdcliffe Colony, ultimately became disillusioned by the structure Whitehead had imposed at Byrdcliffe. Seeing such structure as an impediment to the creative spirit, White left Byrdcliffe and, with Fritz van der Loo, purchased fifteen hundred acres of land just over the Woodstock town line for $2,000. In many respects, the Maverick Festivals, as chronicled by Robinson in the following essay, became a precursor to the Woodstock Festival—both in spirit and energy. As a testament to White's vision, the Maverick Concerts still operate each summer within the framework of the 1916 concert hall he constructed. Esteemed by all who met him, Hervey White—and his giving nature—remains one of the more beloved figures in Woodstock history.

Bolton Brown once remarked in the course of one of his philosophic monologues that the Maverick was a state of mind rather than a geographic subdivision of Woodstock. As usual, Bolton was right, for, as a matter of fact, the Maverick is not in Woodstock at all. If it were, the political history of our town might be rather different than it is, but since the independent spirits who inhabit the Maverick are officially registered as citizens of West Hurley, we have practically nothing to say about what goes on in Woodstock. Woodstock, however, has plenty to say about what goes on at the Maverick.

Hervey White, founder of the Maverick Art Colony.

The Maverick

It is all libelous, of course. I would not sully the pages of our learned historical journal by enumerating some of the charges leveled against us by our property-holding brethren in Woodstock. The magazine of fantasy is just about exhausted whenever the Maverick is mentioned, and *raconteurs* out-vie each other in relating their particular purple experience at such and such a festival, or So-and-So's party. I believe a truth is being stated here for the first time when I say that the Mavericks are a highly domesticated, hardworking group of *petit bourgeois* whose problems happen to lie in the particular regions of music, paint and literature. Anything else is a foul canard. If there are bushes on the place, that is the fault of nature, not of the happily married folk who live there.

The history of the Maverick is, of course, the history of Hervey White. When, as a young idealist, he enlisted under the banner of Ralph Whitehead to found Byrdcliffe, he already had a deep-rooted desire to establish an arts and crafts colony of his own. It was no disloyalty to Ralph Whitehead to entertain such a dream. This is scarcely the place to compare or contrast the two individuals who are largely responsible for the up-bubbling of art that goes on in these hills, but it can be said with perfect frankness that they were of different origins and backgrounds, separated by a whole world of economic difference, and destined, each in his own way, to work out the ideal vision he beheld. Hervey White has always been a poor man; he could not be Hervey White and be any other kind of man. It was only natural, then, when he undertook to project his own personality in the forming of a Utopian colony, that this colony should be projected, financed and forwarded on a scale less grand than the Byrdcliffe experiment.

Actually, Hervey White had to borrow $1,000 to gain title to the region now known as the Maverick. It was the farm of Peter Ostrander, 102 acres lying on the Glenford Turnpike on the south side of Mount Ohio, at an approximate distance of two and a half miles southwest of the village of Woodstock. The farm had a single house, a substantial building that still stands; there were also cows, chickens and pigs, and a mortgage. The mortgage is still unpaid, although the cows and pigs have long been supplanted by other tenants. Practically everyone in the Maverick has lived in the Ostrander farmhouse at one time or another.

Hervey had a partner in this venture of purchasing a farm, a young Hollander named van der Loo, who thought for a while that he wanted to lead a Utopian existence of simple living and high thinking. But van der Loo was not able to live off lentil soup and Ruskin indefinitely, so he took himself off to Holland to find a stout Dutch bride and good Amsterdam fare. Before he went, however, he and Hervey entered into a compact that has kept the Maverick all in one piece. Briefly, they agreed never to sell an inch of the Maverick without the consent of both parties—Hervey and Fritz. And they further agreed *never* to give their consent. It works this way: If Hervey weakens when someone offers him a good round sum for a chunk of Maverick soil, he always says, "Cable Fritz van der Loo for his consent." The cable is sent, and the answer always comes back, "Nothing doing." Once, however, Carl Walters really got serious about buying the land on which his kiln and house are situated. He wanted to buy about three acres from Hervey, and Hervey wanted him to have it. But the old formula had to be used: "Cable Fritz." Carl sent the cable, and the answer came back. "Will sell at $5,000 an acre." This so cooled our leading ceramist and glassmaker that he never mentioned the subject again.

The first artists on the Maverick were musicians, and the first musician to settle there was Paul Kefer. Later, Pierre Henrotte and the elder Barzin came, and there was much informal music on the Maverick during the years 1909–12. Even Hervey used to play a fiddle. Yes, according to his own story, he was quite a fiddler of barn dance music—but, as one can imagine, this did not blend with the nobler type of chamber music that Kefer, Henrotte and Barzin made. So Hervey stepped into the background as always, and let the artists do their ensemble stuff for larger and larger groups of music lovers. The first real concert took place in Firemen's Hall, shortly after the beginning of the World War in 1914. Under the leadership of Pierre Henrotte and the elder Leon Barzin, a concert was given by Maverick musicians for the benefit of the starving Belgians. It was a tremendous success and sowed the germ of the ensemble idea in Hervey's head. In 1916, he built the music hall and thus founded a home for the annual series of concerts that have shed considerable renown on Woodstock as a musical center.

Now for the oft-repeated story of the festival. It seems unbelievable that everybody hasn't heard it, but here it goes for the records. Early in 1915, Hervey was forced to dig a well to supply water to the group of houses around "Birdseye." The well drillers sunk their shafts in the ledge mountainside and for fifteen hundred feet encountered nothing but good, tough bluestone. Now, bluestone can be an embarrassing mineral when you are drilling through it at $1 a foot, and at the end of the drilling operation Hervey found himself faced with a bill of $1,500. By this time the Maverick was beginning to be valued for its contributions to Woodstock life, and out of friendship for Hervey a group of artists decided to settle the well driller's bill by putting on some kind of festive, dramatic production. This performance, destined to go down in history as the First Festival, was held in a bluestone quarry on Hervey's property and, according to some, was the best festival ever held.

For those attending the Maverick Festival, a lack of inhibition was a requirement.

At any rate, it put off the well drillers until the next year when there was another festival, which was also a great success. Hervey thus found himself with a rather important source of income, and for fifteen years the festival gave him his principal revenue. The festival idea expanded enormously; it became the only thing of its kind in America, a frankly bacchanalian rout at which most of the ordinary inhibitions were slipped off, revealing the merrymakers as something the Greeks had plenty of words for. As many as five thousand revelers sometimes cooked their campfire dinners, saw Hervey's show and made the surrounding mountainside ring with the sound of their merriment—into which, I am sorry to say, crept a sinister note of brawling and alcoholism. Finally, no woman's honor, or no man's teeth or nose, were quite safe, and more in sorrow than in anger, Hervey was obliged to discontinue the festival in 1931.

One of the memorable post-festival sights was a lineup of creditors at his house the next day. The local grocery man, butcher, lumber dealer and builder were on hand just as Hervey finished his morning coffee. They stood in a long line, presented their bills and Hervey paid them in spot cash. I have seen him start the day with $3,500 and at nightfall he would not have a penny. He was, however, all set for another year of feeding and housing people, helping them out of tough spots and as nearly as possible proving that his personal gain was the last thing in the world to be considered.

The "painter element" was late in arriving at the Maverick. Long before the triumphal entry of Harry Gottlieb into the promised valley (1921), Hervey's settlement had been overrun by a group of literary personalities. Under Hervey's editorship, they had put out a splendid magazine called the *Plowshare* between 1915 and '16. Allen Updegraff, Edwin Bjorkman, Gustave Hellstrom and Harold Ward were among the contributors to this excellent little periodical, now being revived under the editorship of Hervey White, Henry Morton Robinson and Ernest Brace. But the painters began coming after the war, and with their superabundant vitality began to overwhelm the effete writing crowd. Such burly specimens as Arnold Blanch, Austin Mecklem and Carl Walters set foot upon this writers' Eden and proceeded to make it famous for its red barns, pottery pigs, scraggly pines and undulating landscape. A sculptor, one John Flanagan, being out of work one day, seized an axe, felled a native chestnut and with immortal strokes proceeded to carve out the wooden horse that has become the

Hervey White (back row, left) with more Maverick revelers.

symbol of Hervey White's colony. For this rough-hewn masterpiece, on which he used no tools but an axe, he received fifty cents an hour, which in addition to room and board is mighty good pay for any kind of artwork—if you could get it anytime you needed it.

Other Maverick artists have received larger awards, however. No fewer than three Guggenheim Fellowships have been won by them since 1930. Henry Gottlieb, Arnold Blanch and Lucille Blanch have not only won these fellowships, but a number of other signal honors have been bestowed upon them by juries and museums. Arnold Blanch hangs in the Metropolitan, Carl Walters made the unique glass doors for the Whitney Museum and A.G. Arnold is becoming one of the best lithographers in the country. Among the younger crop of American painters, Wendell Jones and Eugene Ludins are very much in the forefront of things. All these are permanent residents on the Maverick, and their achievements must be reckoned as part of the influence that the Maverick is having on contemporary art.

But lest it be thought that painters and painting, music and musicians, writers and writing are monopolizing Hervey's affections, we must remember the theatre, built in 1924. It is difficult to say exactly what Hervey planned for his playhouse, but if anyone ever caught a glimpse of the barrelful of play manuscripts that Hervey has on his premises, it would he fairly easy to surmise that Hervey built the theatre as an outlet for his own unpublished plays. Architecturally, Hervey did very well by the theatre. It was a huge, rustic edifice with a seating capacity of one thousand, and a stage completely equipped with all modern apparatus. The first year an eminently successful company, including such well-known actors as Dudley Digges, Helen Hayes, Charles McArthur and Edward G. Robinson, put on a series of fine dramatic productions, notably *The Dragon*. The subsequent fortune of the theatre has been various. One year it was reduced to casting the present writer as leading man, with results that did not precisely advance the cause of American drama. Later, there was a much more brilliant year with Gladys Hurlburt and a very hectic season with a young gentleman named Russell Wright. The last two or three years have been moderately successful from a financial point of view, but somehow we cannot help feeling that the theatre has not attained the high artistic goal that Hervey set for it. Only one of his own plays has been produced here, *The Blizzard* in 1926. Like all practical philosophers, Hervey has accommodated himself to the situation and secured a small but steady revenue from the theatre every year.

Thus far we have enumerated in some detail the many activities that take place in the valley of squinting windows, as Farrell Pelly once called the Maverick. But what about the underlying philosophy, the motivating energy that makes the Maverick like no other region in the world? The answer to these questions may be found in the personality of Hervey White himself. To capture the elements of that personality and to project them in language would be a task requiring the combined efforts of a poet, a psychoanalyst and a discerning friend, preferably one who has sat with Hervey through countless long winter evenings before his fireplace, been silent with him as a log crumbled to glowing ash or heard him read the poets that he loves best: Swinburne, Rosetti, Dante, all memories of his youth, when the pre-Raphaelite wave washed the world and Idealism was the strongest form of reality. At such times, Hervey's romanticism, mixed with a tender paternalistic strength, is found to be deep and enduring in his life attitude. Yet he never permits either of these emotions to get sticky. Somewhere in Hervey White is a good, tough strain of practicality, and a subdued note of fatalism, both of which save him from grieving over lost things, disappointments long endured or the aggression of exploiters. It all came out last summer when a neighbor of Hervey's asked to be allowed to use the name "Maverick" for a swimming pool in the vicinity. Hervey agreed, and even consented to dedicate the pool. In the briefly ironic speech at the dedication, Hervey said:

> *I have been accused of softness in letting another man use the word "Maverick" as the name of his amusement park. Well, this is what I say: A Maverick is anyone's property—anyone who can capture and hold it, can have it. If another man wishes to try it, good luck to him, but I know it would be easier to steal Hercules' club than to attempt the proprietorship of something that is as free as the air, as restless as the wind.*

THE WOODSTOCK DRESS

From HSW Archives

When we think of fashion in relation to Woodstock, most people, no doubt, conjure up images of tie-dyed shirts and faded jeans. Long before the hippie "uniform" made an appearance on the streets of Woodstock, however, Augusta Allen's Woodstock Dress was the fashion of the day when it came to attending social functions or going about everyday tasks.

Along with her husband Willard, Augusta Allen arrived in Woodstock not long after artists had laid claim to the town. Willard, a well-to-do man at the time, desired to be an artist and, in pursuit of that dream, gave up his work in Ohio to bring his family to Woodstock. After building two large homes overlooking the village and acquiring a large tract of land within the village, financial setbacks soon had the Allen family struggling to support their way of life in Woodstock. So it was, out of economic necessity, that Augusta Allen began the design and creation of the Woodstock Dress in 1917. Mrs. Allen was a hardworking woman and, through the creation and sale of her dresses, saw a way to pay for the coal they needed to heat the family home. Already an accomplished seamstress, she designed the dress pattern and went to work sewing at her kitchen table. Family members recall hearing the treadle sewing machine "whirring" all night long. Her daughter, Ruth Greenwood Brown, assisted by creating many of the handmade buttonholes.

The dresses were made of cotton, velvet, taffeta and other select types of fabric, and it wasn't long before the Woodstock Dress was in high demand by Woodstock women. The dresses were worn on many different occasions. It

Willard and Augusta Allen pose in front of their Woodstock home. *Photo courtesy of Fred and Gloria Allen.*

Every Saturday, residents and visitors alike arrived at the center of Woodstock for the Woodstock Market Fair. It is here that Augusta Allen first sold her Woodstock Dress.

The Woodstock Dress

Augusta Allen's Woodstock Dress, as presented at a recent Historical Society of Woodstock exhibit. *Photo by Richard Heppner.*

could, for example, be a casual everyday dress to wear to the post office or to the market. It was a favorite of females within the art colony and was worn by many of the Cheats and Swings square dancers during their exhibition dances in the 1930s and early 1940s. On one such occasion, as legend has it, the group performed for President Roosevelt and his wife Eleanor at Hyde Park. The "spirits" served that evening, however, eventually got the better of two of the dancers. So it was, by evening's end, that the Woodstock Dress had its first test as a bathing suit as the dancers found themselves upended in the Roosevelt swimming pool. On a more positive note, one of Mrs. Allen's dresses is also known to have won first prize on a ship bound for Europe.

In the early 1920s, Mrs. Allen also made costumes for different balls and the Maverick Festivals. She was an active member of the Guild of Craftsmen and one of the first to display her work at the Woodstock Market Fair. Every Saturday during the summer season, you would find her beautiful dresses and aprons on sale in the center of town. Her Tyrolean skirts, blouses and quilted jackets with silver buttons were also very popular. The dresses were sold for $25.00 and her aprons went for $1.50.

As is often found when examining the unique chapters within Woodstock's larger story, the Woodstock Dress represents yet another instance when creativity combined with necessity to offer a distinct contribution to the character of Woodstock life.

Homeland Security— Woodstock during the First Months of World War II

By Richard Heppner

Editor's Note: Throughout the years following the arrival of artists in Woodstock, the town was often a divided entity. Old ways and new ideas often collided at every intersection. In many respects, it took a world war to begin reversing the ill will many harbored toward the "other side." This essay, which appeared in the 2007 edition of the Publications of the Historical Society of Woodstock, *focuses on that reversal, as townspeople from all sectors came together as never before in common cause.*

When the phone rang in the homes of Joseph Friedenberg, Bruno Zimm and Harry Kutzschblack on the morning of December 8, 1941, there was little surprise when the voice on the other end identified himself as calling from Mitchell Field in New York. Nor were they surprised when they were instructed by the caller to be "on the lookout for all suspicious planes and to report them immediately to Mitchell Field." Less than twenty-four hours had passed since Woodstock's quiet Sunday afternoon had been dramatically interrupted by the news that the Japanese had bombed Pearl Harbor. With three phone calls, World War II had come to Woodstock.

Like other Woodstockers that day, Woodstock's three air raid wardens— Friedenberg, Zimm and Kutzschblack—went on to carry out their duties as assigned. Gathering their appointed assistants, the three met to develop plans that would ensure that the geographic sectors they represented, Ohayo Mountain, Lewis Hollow and Lake Hill, would have at least one lookout on duty at all times.

Meanwhile, Woodstock's supervisor, Albert Cashdollar, was also busy—but not necessarily with the daily business of the town. Rather, Cashdollar, who also headed the Ulster County Defense Council, was attempting to arrange a meeting for that evening in Kingston. His primary focus for that evening's meeting would be to distribute enrollment forms to town representatives for the purpose of registering citizens who could aid in "any way" with the defense of Ulster County.

Cashdollar's meeting meant that Warren Hutty's evening would also see him traveling to Kingston. Hutty, who served as the temporary defense chairman for Woodstock, would further learn that, in addition to registering Woodstockers as part of the county's defense plan, he would need to call a meeting "as soon as possible" of Woodstock's health, highway, elected officials and others to oversee defense plans for Woodstock and to elect a permanent chairman who would organize and lead those efforts. Hutty would waste little time, as the registration of Woodstockers able to aid in the defense of the town began almost immediately. Within one week of Pearl Harbor, registration was in full swing and, by the following Wednesday, 160 Woodstockers had signed up to support the town's defense efforts.

On December 20, more than two hundred Woodstockers gathered at town hall and unanimously supported the selection of Martin Comeau to head Woodstock's defense efforts. Those gathered at the meeting, still reeling from the events of the past two weeks, felt little inhibition that evening when it came to expressing their patriotic feelings. The meeting began with the assembly joining Mrs. William Elwyn on piano in the singing of "America." Following the song, Mrs. Arthur Pepper led the room in the Pledge of Allegiance. Prior to concluding the evening by singing the National Anthem, Comeau urged "that all persons—both male and female—between the ages of 16 and 65 register to aid the home defense effort." As if to make it almost impossible to find an excuse for not registering, Comeau, in his first act as chairman, announced that town hall would be open from 9:00 a.m. to 8:00 p.m. Monday through Saturday, and from 12:00 p.m. to 8:00 p.m. on Sundays, for anyone wishing to register. Going even further, and putting his money where his mouth was—so to speak—Comeau announced that he would donate the use of his building next to town hall to serve as Woodstock's defense office. So it was, with the addition of a stove, some office equipment and a telephone (Woodstock 413), that Comeau and his "staff" took up residence there as 1941 neared its close.

As defense chairman, however, Comeau knew he would need more than an office and a phone; he also needed committed individuals to lead Woodstock's efforts in support of the war. So as the holidays passed, Comeau

Martin Comeau headed Woodstock's defense efforts during the course of World War II.

tapped a number of his neighbors to oversee the efforts of the now 317 Woodstockers who had registered to support the town's defense efforts. To begin with, Alice Henderson was selected as chair of food and shelter defense efforts; Dr. Hans Cohn would serve as health officer, with Isabel Doughty serving as his assistant. Theron Lasher would lead the Auxiliary Police force, which included oversight of all air raid wardens. (Initially, Comeau and Lasher divided the town along the lines of the two existing election districts. Responsibility for each district was then assigned to a lieutenant who reported to Lasher. Under the plan, lieutenants would supervise "one to ten squads of four men each," with each squad headed by a sergeant.)

Air raid wardens in the village were led by Reverend Harvey Todd from the Dutch Reformed Church. Working under Todd were Reverend Lester Haws of the Woodstock Methodist Church and Reverend A. Walter Baker of the Christ Lutheran Church. Also serving in the village were William Reilly, Ernest Brace, Andrew Telisky and Adolph Heckeroth, who would also oversee street lighting. Why so many members of the clergy serving as air raid wardens? While Comeau hoped that air raid sirens might, at some point, be set up in different parts of town to sound the alarm, church bells, for the time being, would have to do as Woodstock's initial warning system. Comeau was also mindful of the need for coverage in Woodstock's outlying districts. To that end, Newton Reynolds and Virgil Van Wagonen were appointed to serve as wardens in Bearsville. Craig Vosburgh served in Shady; Egbert Shultis, Lake Hill; William Van Wagner, Willow; Floyd Stone, Wittenberg; Aurel Holumzer, Zena; and George Mayhew, Montoma.

Other assignments would follow from Comeau. Albert Cashdollar would remain as chief of the Woodstock Fire Department. Reginald Lapo would serve as assistant chief. Joesph Hutty, Superintendent of highways, would serve as chief of the Public Works Service, which included oversight of a Demolition and Clearance Squad and a Road Repair Squad.

At the same time, but on a larger scale, Albert Cashdollar, in his role as county chairman, was also busy filling numerous positions countywide. For one important appointment, however, he looked to his hometown and, on January 9, announced the appointment of Woodstock artist Carl Lindin to the Ulster County Tire Rationing Board. Lindin, along with his fellow board members, was presented with the responsibility of doling "out the limited number of new automobile tires" allotted to Ulster County towns outside of Kingston. During the month of January, for example, the Tire Rationing Board began the process of overseeing the disbursement of 299 tires. Of those 299 tires, only 70 were available to the general public. The remaining tires were earmarked for distribution to heavy truck and bus operators. For a resident of Woodstock to receive a new tire he would need a "qualified garage mechanic" to certify that "no more wear remains on the present tire or tires." Once that certification was obtained, however, there was no guarantee that a tire would be forthcoming. The resident seeking a tire would then have to convince the rationing board that his vehicle was necessary for local defense efforts. There is no record indicating the number of "new" friends Carl Lindin might have acquired during this period.

By February 1942, blackout tests became a part of the Woodstock war experience. The first such test came on Monday, February 16, with Woodstock receiving high marks (100 percent perfect performance) for its first effort. During the initial test, fifty-one auxiliary policemen were on duty throughout the town. Just as in the movies, their purpose was to warn residents if any light was escaping from their home. As a local paper noted, "In the village square it was impossible for persons to recognize one another, even at short range, so complete was the blackout."

Woodstock's blackout tests would become a bit more imaginative just a few months later when, on a Thursday evening during the first week in May, a "summons over the telephone to the OCD [Office of Civilian Defense] that the Bearsville Store had been hit by an incendiary bomb" launched Woodstockers into action. Immediately, two ambulances were dispatched. In actuality, however, they weren't really ambulances in the traditional sense. Rather, the vehicles that saw action that evening included Fred Mower's panel truck, with Jack Munday at the wheel, and the Fitzpatrick's family station wagon, driven by Mrs. Fitzpatrick herself. Reaching the scene in just seven minutes, two "victims" were given first aid by Frielan Van De Bogart and Virgil Van Wagonen before they were transported back to the Woodstock Casualty Station, where Dr. Cohn and nurses Lilian Brinkman, Neva Shultis and Edith Blazy waited.

All in all, it proved to be a successful test—with one exception. It seems that, for the Fitzpatrick station wagon, there was a twenty-five-minute delay in Bearsville. Apparently, despite the best-laid plans, no one had accounted for the need to remove the back seat prior to placing a "victim" on a stretcher in the car. As a result, valuable time was lost at the scene as workers endeavored to remove the back seat from Mrs. Fitzpatrick's wagon.

Woodstock had never been known as a town of all work and no play and, despite a world war, resourceful Woodstockers managed to combine their social lives with efforts to provide for the common defense. Perhaps the earliest effort was a Red Cross Waltz ball held in January 1942 at the Woodstock Town Hall. As part of the national defense effort, all local Red Cross chapters were assigned a fundraising goal in support of the national goal of $50 million. Locally, Woodstock's share of that goal was $2,500. By all accounts, the initial fundraising effort was a resounding success. More than four hundred people jammed the town hall that evening, dancing to three different orchestras. The evening's primary fundraising effort was an auction of posters created by Woodstock artists. By evening's end, $841 had been raised.

Only a month later, a Valentine Ball helped push the local chapter of the Red Cross past its $2,500 goal. The ball, chaired by local artist and writer Marion Bullard, "attracted one of the largest crowds ever to assemble at Town Hall," and, according to one account, "It was a gay party and those who attended pronounced it one of the best ever held." Programs for the event were designed by noted children's book authors Maud and Miska Petersham. The evening's entertainment reached its peak with the premiere of Vladimir Pawa's newest composition, the "Woodstock Polka."

In addition to Woodstock artists Lindin, Pawa, the Petershams and Bullard, other artists with connections to Woodstock also found their lives redirected during the first few months of the war. In one of the more ironic twists, painter and lithographer Yasuo Kuniyoshi, despite his status as an alien due to his Japanese heritage, freelanced as a writer of American propaganda broadcasts into Japan. Kuniyoshi, whose wartime work was the subject of an article in the *New Yorker* at the time, was cited by the magazine as "one Japanese we've heard of doing his damnest to help us win the war." While Kuniyoshi's "alien status" prevented him from being directly employed by the Office of the Coordinator of Information in Washington, his scripts were produced on a freelance basis and then delivered to staff members within the Information Office. Despite his wartime efforts on behalf of the United States, Kuniyoshi, also an avid photographer, had his Leica camera taken from him for the "duration of the war." Additionally, since his status prevented him from becoming an American citizen at the time, he was similarly blocked from having his work purchased by the Metropolitan Museum in New York. At the time, the museum's guidelines restricted all purchases to American citizens only.

Woodstock's cultural scene was further diminished with the start of the war when Clifford Richter, who only the summer before had conducted a series of successful Bach concerts with the Maverick Chorus, found himself writing to a local paper from Kelly Field in Texas following his enlistment in the air service. Taking time out during his training to write friends back east, Richter wrote, "Bach must wait until we have won the war." Still, despite the way his artistic life had been redirected, Richter was sustained by his Woodstock experiences. "I am constantly reminded," he continued, "of the music the Maverick Chorus has performed these past two years and from this I receive great courage."

During times of war, resources once taken for granted are often found to be in short supply. As a result, those who remain at home are forced to adapt and seek new solutions in an effort to sustain their own existence. Such was the case with the phenomena known as Victory Gardens. During World War II, according to the Smithsonian Museum, "nearly 20 million" Americans planted victory gardens. As a result, "their efforts growing and preserving their own food saved the nation's war products for the armed forces and Allies." During the early days of World War II, a number of Woodstockers were counted among the ranks of those Americans who undertook their own efforts in pursuit of fresh vegetables.

As the winter that began the war turned toward spring, Martin Comeau appointed Harrison Dowd to head the Woodstock Gardening Committee. With his appointment, Dowd immediately began to organize local efforts on two levels: making parcels of land available for planting and, at the same time, securing seeds and vegetable seedlings for growing.

On the first front, Dowd found Woodstockers extremely generous. Within a short time of initiating the program, landowners throughout town began to donate parcels of land for use by their neighbors. Beginning with a plot of land donated by Martin Comeau running along Route 212 in Bearsville, the program expanded to include parcels of land, for example, at Byrdcliffe. There, Peter Whitehead, son of Byrdcliffe founder Ralph Whitehead, offered a one-hundred- by sixty-foot plot of land behind the Chase cottage on Glasco Turnpike for planting. Elsewhere along Glasco Turnpike, Miss Alice Wardwell made three quarters of an acre available, while Margeret Kenyon also offered a plot of land behind her home.

In Zena, Mrs. Lucy Brown provided area residents with an acre of land on her property. Elsewhere, Milton Chase donated space on Ohayo Mountain Road, while Mrs. Agnes Anderson also offered an acre of land for planting in Bearsville. In the meantime, a number of Woodstockers, such as Mr. and Mrs. Walter McTeague, combined with neighbors to share their backyards, side yards or the fields nearby to expand the potential harvest that would follow.

Under Dowd's leadership, Woodstock also began to offer a seed and plant exchange. A number of Woodstockers helped to get the program off the ground by donating young seedlings for distribution. Included among the early donors were Mrs. Joseph Hutty, Anita Smith, Margaret Kenyon and Victor Cannon. Cannon, who would later be honored by the town for his support of the victory garden program, also volunteered the use of his tractor (with an operator) to those making use of the town's community gardens. In addition to the seedlings, Marion Bullard and Ben Webster were early providers of seeds to the gardening program as well.

In an effort to ensure the success of the victory gardens, Dowd and his committee also focused on providing residents with the information needed to become successful gardeners. To that end, a number of lectures and demonstrations were offered to the public that focused on proper planting techniques, how to can and properly store vegetables and the proper use of pesticides.

By all accounts, the victory garden program in Woodstock was successful in meeting its goal of providing town residents with fresh vegetables made scarce by the war. At a time when the nation's harvest was surely taxed by the government's efforts to feed both American and Allied troops, Woodstockers came together to ensure that they would not be without fresh tomatoes, cucumbers, beets, carrots, lettuce, snap beans, radishes, peppers, corn, squash and even watermelons. Yet, while the main purpose of the program was to bring fresh vegetables to Woodstock tables, Woodstock's victory gardens, in the mind of Harrison Dowd, served an even higher, patriotic purpose. As Dowd offered, in an announcement to the local paper, "Get away from the radio, the headlines, the rumor-spreaders, and see what the combination of seed and soil can do for you. We at home can fight the war our own way; not by arm chair strategy, not by lying awake and speculating, certainly not by rumor spreading or listening, but by keeping one's mind and body fit for whatever may come. For this, gardening is the best answer."

The rationing of tires and gas, and the need to plant and grow victory gardens, speaks to the demands of a war machine that, when directed toward fighting a global war, draws supplies and material into it much like a black hole. As a result, Woodstock, like most towns and cities across the nation, was impressed with the need to support the call for material that would assist in the continuous feeding of that machine. In an effort to do so, the Office for Civilian Defense appointed Reverend A. Walter Baker to head up the town's salvage efforts. According to Baker, the importance of a successful salvage effort in Woodstock was threefold. First, a successful salvage effort offered "immediate value to munitions makers, by permitting the manufacturing of munitions more easily than having to draw from raw materials." In addition, the "recycling" of salvage material would go far in alleviating anticipated shortages while, at the same time, providing citizens with the "opportunity to do something towards winning the Victory." As a result, Baker, and the committee he led, set out to lead the salvage effort throughout

Woodstock. Most sought after were such items as papers, magazines, iron and other metals, rubber, paste, rags of all kinds, burlap, soap and toothpaste tubes.

To facilitate the collection of items, two large "stall areas," provided by William Elwyn, were set up in sheds near the Reformed Church, just off the Village Green. Larry Goetz was appointed "salvage master," with the task of "sorting and bundling the material" that would eventually be hauled to Kingston. Woodstockers unable to drop off their items in the village were asked to have a neighbor deliver the material for them. Additionally, local grocers, such as the Bearsville Store, Happys or William Mower's store, offered, when delivering groceries, to pick up their customers' salvage material and drop it off on their return to town. Finally, should all else fail, both Office of Civilian Defense volunteers and members of the Boy Scouts could be called upon to assist in getting items delivered to the salvage center.

Once situated in the center of Woodstock, Happy's general store not only delivered groceries to Woodstockers but also would often return with items donated by customers for the town's salvage effort.

Once shipped to Kingston, the salvage material was sold to authorized dealers. What money was generated from the sale was then used to defray the expenses of the Civilian Defense Office, the Boy Scouts or the local chapter of the Red Cross.

Finally, the story of Woodstock's homeland security efforts during the months immediately following Pearl Harbor ends where it began, with the eyes of Woodstockers gazing upward in search of enemy planes. Not long after the war began, and in an effort to improve upon the town's "spotting" efforts, the Woodstock Observation Post was established at Anita Smith's Stonecrop home at the base of Overlook Mountain.

Appointed as "Chief Observer," Smith oversaw the building of a unique element of Woodstock's war efforts. Operationally, the observation post began simply enough, with spotters sitting in a field gazing skyward. A telephone in a nearby shed served as the means to report any sightings made. By the summer of 1942, however, through donations and fundraisers, a wooden tower was erected to provide relief from the elements for more than one hundred volunteer spotters. During its construction, a four-leaf clover for good luck was placed under one of the stones that formed the tower's foundation. Staffed twenty-four hours a day, through bitter winter nights and the heat and humidity of summer, the volunteers dutifully noted every plane that passed overhead. As described by Gladys Hurlburt, who also served as publicity director for the post, the Woodstock post was part of a "vast system of national Air Defense, now known as The First Fighter Command." Hurlburt also noted the importance of such a post in Woodstock: "It is a mistake to think of Woodstock as remote and out of danger. As bombers fly, we are fifteen minutes from the heart of New York. When New York is attacked, the enemy planes will scatter…They will get rid of their bombs wherever they are. When they try to get away from our planes, we go into action. We keep the army informed of the directions of their flights."

While the nature of their work was of extreme importance, the life of a spotter at Stonecrop mixed brief flurries of activity with a great deal of time to simply ponder the war and life in Woodstock. A typical early morning stint as a spotter was described in June 1942 by Woodstock artist Allen Cochran:

> *Twelve, Midnight: I look at the bulletin board, "Special Instructions for reporting suspicious incidents." It brings the gooseflesh. Beautiful night. Hope it's as clear as this over Germany. "Go get 'em RAF!"*

One A.M.: Everything under control. There goes a car. Good night, who ever you are! A rooster crows. At this hour? He must be cockeyed.

Two A.M.: Halfway mark. Coffee from my thermos. It's certainly quiet. A mouse in the wall sounds more like a cow. What? What's that? I hear a plane. I search the sky. A star moves. There it is! I report it. "Flash—to the east and going south." Man's voice answers from New York. Crisp but nice. Stillness again.

Three A.M.: Wonder where that plane was going? Wonder if anyone else is awake in the village? On nights like this, no one sleeps in Malta or Dover, or, I hope, in Tokyo. I hope Mr. Goering drops in here. Where's my pitchfork? "Flash! I wish to report Herman Goering plumping down on our meadow." Oh I wish it very much.

Four A.M.: Bruno Zimm takes over. I drive home in the first light of the morning. Strange hopes for today. I never thought I'd go to sleep saying, "God bless Stalin and Chiang Kai-Shek."

While the observation post was decommissioned two years later, it serves as a reminder—and as a representative centerpiece—for understanding the dedication Woodstockers possessed during this time of sacrifice. Not only was it a place where townspeople and artists alike came together for a common purpose, but it also symbolized Woodstock's connection to a wider world that, at the moment, had gone quite insane. While Woodstockers lived within the apparent safety and protection of the Catskill Mountains, those who looked to the sky each day also knew how quickly that insanity could be visited upon our eastern shores. The war was very real and its outcome quite uncertain. In one of her more poignant recollections of the post's activities, Gladys Hurlburt underscored that connection while, at the same time, offering an image of Woodstock that we all choose to remember. It is an image that provides an explanation, as if one were needed, for the commitment each volunteer brought to his task as the war closed in around them. Upon hearing of the news one morning that described the obliteration of a small Bohemian town, Hurlburt wrote:

This was to be a news column. It was to be gossipy and gay. About the new spotters, Engleburt Roentgen, Peter Whitehead, Margaret Wetterau, Clara Chichester, Mrs. Berlin and Mrs. Lerman of Library Lane. It was to be about the fine, great coat that Alan Waterous gave us. A "linesman coat" he

Memorial Day in Woodstock. Each year, Woodstock takes time out to honor the nation's war dead with a parade through the center of town.

called it. Football trappings enlisted for the duration. We were going to tell about the fireflies. How they bewitch us these nights. We watch a sky full of stars and suddenly they seem to dance! We close our eyes and look again. It's the fireflies. A firefly close to you has a green light like the tail light of a plane a thousand feet above us.

This was to be all our column until this morning we read about Lidice. When we got to the Post our youngest spotter was on duty. His name is Dan Randolph and he is twelve years old. He started as an assistant observer but he was so good he was promoted. He knows more about the planes than most grown-ups. He is very proud of his job. At home he draws planes and studies pictures of enemy markings. When a plane flies over his house, he runs out to check it. He writes down slogans. He says his favorites so far are: "Keep 'em Spotted" and "Let's go Spotters!" That morning he stood out in the field looking up. He ran to the telephone when he saw a plane. His face was very serious. When his time was up he got on his bicycle and went home. His mother was waiting for him. She had his dinner ready. He was safe.

Lidice was a town in Bohemia as all the world knows. There is nothing there now. The homes have been burnt. There are no men. They have all been shot. There are no women. They have all been taken to "camps." The children have been placed in "suitable institutions." There is no Lidice today because not one soul would tell if he knew anything about the hero who shot the Nazi hangman, Heydrich.

As Don went home to dinner our village was quiet. Women worked in their gardens. Men went about their business. The mail came in. The little Carey boy ran his fire engine up and down in front of his father's store. It looked like any summer day. But it was not. Something was happening to all of us. A rage was swelling in us as we thought about the children of Lidice crying for their mothers. Woodstock is about the same size as Lidice.

That summer, Woodstockers gathered to celebrate the first Fourth of July since Pearl Harbor. As the crowd gathered around the speakers' platform on the Village Green, they were welcomed by the Woodstock Drum Corps, which, as the newspaper noted, "never played with more vim and precision." Reverend Todd served as master of ceremonies and Dr. James Shotwell, perhaps Woodstock's most noted citizen, spoke. But the highlight of the day was when the crowd surged forward to join Allen Waterous in the singing of "America," "God Bless America" and the "Star Spangled Banner."

Homeland Security

Less than two weeks later, many in that Independence Day crowd also joined in a Bastille Day celebration held at town hall. Organized by the Free French Movement in Woodstock, music again served to unite those gathered. As Myrett Ponsella, a singer of Paris street songs who, only weeks earlier, had escaped from Nazi-occupied France, wandered through the crowd singing, she paused, slipped the accordion from her shoulders and, with raised arms, led the crowd in singing the "La Marseillaise."

In many respects, this was perhaps a more unique time in Woodstock history than those assembled on the Green or in the town hall that July realized. Woodstock, more than anytime in its history—and perhaps its future—was a united town. There was work to be done and the debates and differences of the past mattered little. More than three years of war would remain.

For many, that spring and summer would be the last they would spend in Woodstock for a while. Draft notices arrived, others enlisted. Their journey toward destinations unknown often began by bus departing from the Village Green. Perhaps, on their way out of town, they passed someone working in a victory garden, or a Boy Scout hauling pieces of scrap metal up the hill. Perhaps the car they saw turning into Rock City Road was on its way to Stonecrop, or to a meeting that would plan the next blackout exercise. Perhaps they saw the Carey boy running his truck up and down the sidewalk. Undoubtedly, they glanced back one more time for a glimpse of Overlook. They, like those who remained behind, would do their part.

Twelve of them would never return.

Author's Note: This essay was based on newspaper accounts from the Historical Society of Woodstock's archives. Unfortunately, the articles used were originally clipped out of newspapers during the war without the name of the newspaper, date or page number included (a lesson to all of us who wish to preserve clippings for future reference). From research, however, it appears that the clippings came from either the Woodstock Press *or the* Ulster County News *(both papers are no longer publishing). Additional reference sources included* Woodstock History and Hearsay *by Anita Smith (WoodstockArts, 2006),* Woodstock, History of a Small Town *by Alf Evers (Overlook Press, 1987) and the Smithsonian Institution (http://americanhistory.si.edu).*

TWINE'S CATSKILL BOOKSHOP AND THE ART OF GROWING UP IN WOODSTOCK

By Tinker Twine

Editor's Note: The following essay pays homage to the arts and literary scene that was so much a part of postwar Woodstock. In addition, the author revises a recent Publications *essay on growing up in Woodstock. While Woodstock would soon collide with the energy of the sixties, Woodstock life in the late 1950s and early 1960s moved at a much slower pace—with little knowledge, or care, about what might be on the horizon.*

My parents' Woodstock store, Twine's Catskill Bookshop, aka Twine's Books, Records and Art Supplies, was a social center for artists and writers. Donald and Elise Twine made it so—from the day they became partners with Dick Burlingame in 1955 until they sold the business in 1978. It was cozy at the store, which always smelled like paint, linseed oil and turpentine. Dogs were welcomed and offered biscuits. Agnes Ridgeway, who wrote scripts for the *Dr. Kildare* TV show, lived in the upstairs apartment.

The Twines were publishers, too. Enamored of Woodstock and proud of its history, they reprinted Will Rose's bittersweet memoir about life in turn-of-the-century Woodstock, *The Vanishing Village*, in 1970. And they revived classics of the public domain, *Picturesque Ulster* and *Enjoying the Catskills*.

Twine's Catskill Bookshop served for many years as a hub for authors and artists alike. *Photo courtesy of Tinker Twine.*

AUTHORS' PARTIES

Watching Donald (father, a W.C. Fields fan) prepare his stealthy planter's punch for authors' parties was a study in opulence. With a quart of Meyer's dark rum in one hand and a half-gallon of pineapple juice in the other, ceremoniously he'd pour some over a mountain of ice cubes in a huge cut glass bowl. There were other ingredients, like champagne, a jar of maraschino cherries, two quarts of ginger ale, triple sec, sprigs of fresh mint and god-knows-what-all. "Ambrosia!" he'd exclaim, tasting it. The guests—friends of the author and anyone else who walked in—apparently agreed. The beverage looked and tasted precious, like refreshment for a ladies' bridge circle; its effects were profound.

Ma kept me busy preparing pickles wrapped in slices of salami secured with toothpicks. Cheese and crackers. Sliced cucumbers on buttered triangles of de-crusted white bread…hors d'oeuvres least likely to cause damage when dropped on a book.

Heywood Hale Broun signs book as Elise Twine looks on. *Photo courtesy of Tinker Twine.*

Along with the Twines, the events were presided over by James Gibson and generations of loyal employees who ranged over the years to include Nancy Summers, Cornelia Hartman, Dorothy LaCasse, Frances Dederick, Eric Angeloch, Sandy Merch, Mindy Dunham, Daisy Jansen and more. (Robert Angeloch, an instructor at the Art Students' League and a customer who visited, coffee in hand, before his class most summer mornings, married Nancy; they produced Eric, who grew up to be a great landscape artist like his parents and his grandparents.) Frances, Cornelia and Mindy were artists, too.

The book signing parties were historic occasions, as in 1970, when Howard and Martha Lewis were honored for their groundbreaking exposé, *The Medical Offenders*, which became a bestseller. Fortunately, photographer Milton Wagenfohr was present at most of these affairs, of which there were twenty-six altogether, starting in 1958 with honoree Robert Phelps. I loved Phelps's novel, *Heroes and Orators*, which was set in Woodstock during the early 1950s and starred recognizable local characters hanging out at the storied Seahorse tavern. The last party was for Heywood Hale Broun (Woodie) in 1978, for his autobiography, *Whose Little Boy Are You?* It was a question posed to him as a child by Eleanor Roosevelt at a party hosted by his parents, columnist Heywood Broun and suffragette Ruth Hale.

Fausto's Keyhole author Jean Arnoldi (attractive wife of artist Fletcher Martin, former wife of musician Frank Mele and mother of Andre Mele) set the stage for one of Twine's most successful parties in 1970. I remember it even though I only heard about it second-hand. Donald was awed to have witnessed a spontaneous pugilistic encounter between Fletcher Martin and abstract painter Bud Plate, both macho he-men. The fight was over a woman, though it wasn't clear which woman. No one was hurt. Not much, anyway. The scene was reminiscent of Martin's artwork. One of his signature themes was the prizefight.

The poet Loker Raley was fêted for his literary journal, *Bluestone*, in 1965. John Pike signed his book of instruction, *Watercolor*, in 1966. In 1972, painter Frank Brockenshaw was photographed seated among four authors: Edgar Pangborn, writer of thrillers including *Good Neighbors and Other Strangers*; David Ballantine, who wrote *Lobo*; and Rick and Glory Brightfield, authors of *Mazes*. *Woodstock Handmade Houses* by Ballantine, Bob Haney and John Elliot, a big hit in the mid-1970s, has become a classic and a source of inspiration for aspiring builders. Architects Jeffrey Milstein and Les Walker also published books that were toasted at Twine's.

Holley Cantine and Dachine Rainer, outspoken conscientious objectors during World War II, made a striking couple. They were pictured at a party for Dachine, who had written the novel *The Uncomfortable Inn* in 1960. Holley was a famous character who in earlier days had published a pamphlet in Woodstock. His most famous headline was "Tourists Go Home!"

Other writers who signed their books at Twine's parties included Howard Koch, Alf Evers, Charles Boswell, Anthony Robinson, Nancy Klein, Helen Wolfert, Roland Van Zandt, Thom Roberts, Peter Lyon, Walter Kortrey and Louise Ault.

While some wrote novels, others were historians. Alf Evers wrote two seminal books: *The Catskills from Wilderness to Woodstock* and *Woodstock, History of a Small Town*. Louise Ault's *Artist in Woodstock* described her late husband, George Ault, and their life here during the 1930s and 1940s. The Phelps book that I love, *Heroes and Orators*, blends fact and fiction about the town and its people. Howard Koch, the screenwriter famous for *As Time Goes By*, was fêted at Twine's for his book, *The Panic Broadcast*, about his believable but fictitious 1930s radio report of Martians landing in New Jersey.

I recently came across a newspaper article, "Book Party Report," written by Peter Moscoso-Gongora in 1974 for the *Woodstock Press*. Here are some excerpts:

Woodstock historian Alf Evers (second from right) signs in the company of (left to right) Barbara Moncure, Elise Twine and Donald Twine. *Photo courtesy of Tinker Twine.*

I was getting high on the radishes. Wherever did Elise Twine get them? Each one was like a double martini. The occasion was Donald Twine's book party for Peter Lyon and his new book, Eisenhower, *so I shouldn't have to tell you what it was about...*

Scholar-Sports Reporter Woody Broun was there with his glamorous wife, Jane. I wanted to ask him whether Ali will beat Foreman (I think he will), but he must get bored by questions like that. The Kalishes were there. Irving was telling me about a time a mysterious lady dropped her handkerchief on Madison Avenue, he picked it up and ran after her, and it turned out to be Greta Garbo. I had an idea that the story continued, but Mrs. Kalish was standing right there...

James Gibson, smiling came up to me and said, "I read your story in Playgirl." "How did you like it?" I asked. "I didn't," he said, still smiling and walked off.*

THE BEGINNING

My earliest memories of the bookshop (before we owned it) were free Candlelight Concerts held in the backyard on summer evenings. Dick Burlingame (later the Twine's partner until 1958) played classical long-playing albums—the technology was new—on a phonograph set on a windowsill. The audience brought snacks and sat on blankets. Citronella candles lent atmosphere and slightly discouraged mosquitoes. Fireflies were abundant. My mother enjoyed the music and brought me with her.

The Twines bought a share of the business a few years later. They had moved from Ellenville to Woodstock in 1949 and rented a Byrdcliffe house (Carniola) the first summer.

Elise was an actress and had performed at the Woodstock Playhouse during the 1940s. She and Jane Lloyd-Jones, from Los Angeles, and Lisa Downer, from Wheeling, West Virginia, had met and become friends in the Drama Department at Carnegie Tech in Pittsburgh in 1941. Later, Jane married Heywood Hale Broun; Lisa married artist Ken Downer. It seemed fateful that the three friends ended up in Woodstock.

Donald, originally from Yonkers, was going stir crazy in Ellenville, my mother's hometown, but he loved Woodstock right away. The store allowed him to stay with his family and to quit his career as a radio operator in the Merchant Marines, which had kept him at sea for months at a time.

The Twines' business partner, Dick Burlingame, was a suave, handsome gentleman who was more popular with the ladies than he cared to be. My parents noticed that when eager females were seen approaching the front door, Dick would climb out the back window. (It was a trick I emulated later as a Twine employee when certain customers revealed their grumpy sides.) Dick lunched regularly with John Pike across the street at Deanie's. Lunch marked the end of Dick's productivity for the day.

We Sold Records, Too

We sold records for several years and joked about one in particular, an album by Julie London called *Misty*. In a pre-adolescent attempt at humor, I remarked to my mother, "Misty's getting pretty dusty." (Ma laughed, a nice change of pace.) In addition to classical albums produced by Angel, we sold Elvis's early records and were in on the phenomenal emergence of Bob Dylan, who spent several years in Woodstock, writing some of his best songs. Cornelia Hartman drew our attention to his records. A hip and cosmopolitan young woman, Cornelia told us he was becoming popular in the coffee houses of Greenwich Village.

Soon Dylan was living in a rambling, rustic house on Byrdcliffe mountain (former art colony founded in 1902 by Ralph Radcliffe Whitehead), and his kids were getting pony rides on my horse, Midnight. A bold female neighbor of ours (name forgotten) borrowed Midnight and rode him up to the Dylans' on a regular basis. She told me Bob wanted to buy Midnight. (No dice was the message I sent back.)

One bright summer day I was riding the horse along Glasco Turnpike near the corner of Upper Byrdcliffe Road, when a motorcycle slowed alongside me. There was a striking brunette smiling broadly at Midnight and me. It was Joan Baez, riding behind Bob! I smiled back, of course.

Anyway, mother got rid of the records while father was laid up in Benedictine Hospital with a broken leg, having been kicked by Midnight.

The Children's Corner

Elise liked kids a lot and set up a cute area she called the children's corner, where they could sit around a little table and read. She hung a portrait of Raggedy Ann, which she had painted herself. (She was a student of Frank Brockenshaw, known as Brock, one of our regular customers.) *Pat the Bunny* was a favorite even then, as were all Dr. Seuss, a book I loved called *Suzuki Bean* and we carried all the *Nancy Drew* and *Hardy Boys* books. And the classics, of course. She also stocked a fascinating collection of Beatrix Potter postcards and miniature art supplies.

There was a little red-haired boy who lived in the neighborhood who spent a lot of time at the store. About six years old at first, Jamie would stop in after school, draw pictures and tell us about his daily experiences. This went on for several years. We were very fond of Jamie. I wonder what became of him?

ARTISTS

A brief, random list of artists we served includes Kurt Sluizer, Milton Avery, Gurdon Howe, Robert Orsini, Nick Buhalis, Rollin Crampton, Richard Crist, Arnold Blanche, Lucille Blanche, Milton Glazer, Manuel Bromberg, Rolph Scarlett, Julio De Diego, Marion Greenwood, Nan Mason, Wilna Hervey (who portrayed Powerful Katrinka in the Toonerville Trolley films of the 1920s), Georgina Klitgaard, Doris Lee, Walter Plate, Anton Refregier, Bernard Steffen, John Taylor, Andre Ruellan, Richard Pantell, Roman Wachtel, Thomas Penning, Charles Ruggles, Franklin Alexander, Anthony Krauss, Calvin Grimm, Reginald Wilson, Carolyn Haeberlin, Ethel Magafan, Bruce Currie, Joan Elliott, Anita Barbour and many more.

Philip Guston, a towering, taciturn figure, bought huge tubes of black paint and the widest brushes possible. Mindy Dunham and I would speculate about what Guston created with those tools, while we ate our lunch— cheeseburgers from Duey's across the street—in front of the TV. (*The Gong Show* came on at noon. Jimmy Gibson teased us for watching it.) My father enjoyed talking to an artist named Bill Lubinsky, who arrived on a horse he tied up outside.

The poet Pearl Bond and artist John Ernst came in sometimes. Pearl remained seated while John shopped for paint. He'd bring his selections back to her for approval. "Oh, John, you don't need that!" she'd say. Or, "That's good."

Paul Arndt, an elderly gentleman, escorted my mother to lunch in Kingston several times; she loved it. Dan Gottschalk was an interesting Thanksgiving guest. The Klitgaards were neighbors who had a second home in the hamlet of Wittenberg and migrated with the seasons. Gurdon Howe drew hilarious Christmas cards with poetry to match.

My father made personal deliveries of art supplies to Konrad Cramer, Elfriede Borkman, Anton Otto Fischer, Henry Mattson and to beautiful, gracious Jane Keefe, who directed the Country Mouse preschool up the hill from our home.

Jane called. "Donald, I need magenta," she wailed, children at her feet. "Of course you do!" he replied, and soon appeared at the door of the Country Mouse, magenta paint in hand.

Many of our customers were students or instructors at the Art Students' League. When the league closed its summer school in Woodstock in the early 1970s, we were sad for more than one reason. The miasma soon lifted, however, when painters Bob Angeloch and Franklin Alexander opened the Woodstock School of Art to take its place. A few years later, Angeloch moved WSA to the historic Art Students' League campus, where the school is well established today.

PASSING THE TORCH

Having turned seventy in 1978, father was weary of keeping inventory. Imagine the details of pen points, pencils and all the different kinds of brushes, not to mention paints and books! It was too daunting for me to consider taking on, even with Jimmy Gibson's help. And so the business was sold.

Paul Solis-Cohen, who bought the store that year, changed its name to Catskill Art and Office. Paul expanded the building in Woodstock and opened new stores in Kingston, Newburgh and Poughkeepsie, all of which flourish to this day. If my Donald and Elise were still alive, they would be amazed to see how the business has grown!

LIFE ON THE SAWKILL

While my parents were busy earning a living, I was mostly free to explore the natural riches of Woodstock on horseback and on foot, imagining I was Pocahontas. The heart of the town is the Sawkill Creek. From its origin at Echo Lake until it enters the town of Kingston, some twenty meandering miles later, the Sawkill has always been the lifeblood of Woodstock, the reason for its existence, a source of fun and artistic inspiration.

Crystal clear rivulets and calm pools provided habitats for wondrous communities of dragonflies, turtles, frogs, fish, butterflies, horseflies and much more than can be recounted here. To this day, I recognize the smell of turtles. Many an innocent babe has been imprinted with joy while playing on the Sawkill's banks of vast bluestone rocks, a colorful variety of pebbles and soft sandy silt. For eons, people, dogs and horses cooled themselves on hot summer days in its generous, cool water.

Looking back to the 1950s, when the town's population was about two thousand, several swimming areas were available to the public. That was before the population burgeoned, houses sprang up in the way and insurance requirements became the sole determinant of our quality of life. (No Trespassing signs were uncommon in Woodstock until the advent of the 1969 Woodstock Festival, which took place an hour and a half away in Bethel.)

SHADY

Perhaps the most beautiful swimming place was in the hamlet of Shady, where the stream emerged ice cold from the steepest slopes of Overlook and Indian Head Mountains. Big rocks provided ample room for picnics and sunbathing alongside shallow passages and deep pools where teenagers perfected their dives and can openers. Toddlers splashed before the adoring eyes of beautiful young mothers who idled away halcyon days sharing grapes and trading recipes for the ubiquitous zucchini, which flourished in every garden.

Over millennia, the rocks of Shady were worn into huge parallel platforms separated by cascades of varying volume and intensity. One waterfall in particular was a popular place to sit while receiving a natural hydro-massage. There was also a waterfall like a flume you could slide down and land in a little "whirlpool." The behinds of many a bathing suit were worn out on that slide!

In the evenings, families gathered for swimming and cookouts. Potatoes baked in hot ashes, barbecued swordfish, boiled sweet corn. The water was clean enough to drink, and skinny-dipping was a possibility. There was nothing quite like the feeling of the Sawkill flowing around one's naked body.

On a hot summer afternoon, you knew you were in Shady when you scrambled down the road embankment and landed—hop!—on the rocks. The temperature changed, and the ions were soothingly negative. The atmosphere was a marketer's dream. A violinist owned the property, and he didn't object to friends enjoying the stream. One friend leads to another, of course, and soon everyone in town was there. Even then, it wasn't unpleasant. There was room enough.

The boom was lowered in the 1960s, when new owners prohibited swimming. Today, I'd do the same. Still, it's eerie to pass the place and hear no joyous shouts, no splashing, no barking dogs and see no people.

APPLE ROCK

The most accessible swimming hole of my childhood, Apple Rock, exists no more. You can see its remains at the west end of the town-owned Comeau property, where erosion from floods and human intervention during the 1970s buried the rock we used to dive from. Now just the top third of the boulder is visible through sand and pebbles. The rock is identifiable by the many initials, hearts and dates that had been carved into it for so many years.

The rock is now located about ten yards from the current channel. Before the 1970s, however, it offered itself as an eight-foot-high peninsula that jutted into a deep pool from the north bank of the stream. There was room for three people to stretch out and sunbathe, and for a steady stream of jumpers and divers to skid past on their way into the water. A rope dangled from an overhanging tree, so those inclined to play Tarzan were able to indulge their fantasies.

A bunch of us Woodstock kids rode our horses daily through the woods to Apple Rock, where we led our mounts into the water to cool off and escape the deerflies. Then we tied them to trees in the shade while we ate sandwiches and daydreamed about a future we assumed would be as idyllic as the present. "We" included Holly and Gail Green, Susie Perlman, Lloyd, Jimmy and Emmy Gibson and some others. (Okay, it wasn't perfect; there were a few fights, a few disagreements, a few insults, the usual developmental process.)

After the flood that changed the course of the Sawkill by Apple Rock, huge trees fell. They lie across the stream to this day. The problem was not helped by the attentions of CETA workers (Jimmy Carter's Comprehensive Education and Training Act), who were dispatched, apparently, to clear the channel east of Yerry Hill Bridge. I saw them at work. Don't drink while bulldozing the Sawkill. Better yet, don't bulldoze the Sawkill!

SULLY'S, BIG DEEP AND TANNERY BROOK

Everyone knows Sully's. It's still there, still enjoyed by people, albeit mostly by guests of the Woodstock Motel, which used to be called the Millstream. Dan Sully was a theatrical producer of the early twentieth century who owned the property long before the motel was built in the 1950s. The bridge that crosses the stream at the corner of Tannery Brook and Millstream Roads was known as Sully's Bridge. It was red and cute. Kids jumped off it into a pool to the south. Before the motel was built, mothers brought their children, and other kids could walk to Sully's. Calm, with a deep pool that gradually becomes shallow, it was ripe for children's dam-building projects, as it is today.

Big Deep, where movie star Lee Marvin and Pam Feeley (who were married many years later) met as teenagers, is owned by the town and is open to the public. For a swimming hole, it's remarkably large. Sheltered by hemlocks, it has a sandy side and a flat rock side, with room for diving and splashing. Dogs abound there. Where else can a bow-wow catch a stick in the water these days? Sometimes it's noisy, but that's life. While an occasional nudist wanders about, no serious crime has been reported. Thank goodness the town had the foresight to preserve a place that's so much a part of Woodstock's history.

Tannery Brook, which joins the Sawkill about a tenth of a mile south of Sully's Bridge, was also popular for swimming during the 1920s, '30s and '40s. Woodstock historian Alf Evers describes a protest one summer when the City of Kingston, which had purchased water rights, tried to ban swimming in the town. The response was a community meeting on the Village Green followed by a march to the stream. Everyone jumped in, clothes and all. The ban failed, but Tannery Brook, unfortunately, became too polluted for swimming. It's better now that we have a sewer system, but property owners aren't inclined to invite the public anymore. Too much liability.

Farther downstream in Zena, 1950s kids rode horses into deep muddy water by the Red Bridge, where the Sawkill rounds the bend into a Kingston reservoir. They all loved it. The largest animals turned into graceful sea horses, swimming in slow motion in water over their heads. Nothing like it on a summer day.

WINTER IN WOODSTOCK

Since the beginning of time, the hill on the Comeau property across from Woodstock Estates (a former picturesque farm, habitat of swans and current site of the post office) has been enjoyed by children who sled or otherwise careen down its snow-covered slope. The scenic promontory has also served as part of a cross-town horse trail that extended from Byrdcliffe to the Riding Club. In the old days, Woodstock's landscape was dotted with skating ponds, cornfields and cows of the black and white variety. As the fields, ponds and cows disappeared, we clung to the past.

Kids were outfitted in clothes from the Bonnie Shop (where Pegasus Shoes is today), or from London's in Kingston. Speaking of London, we watched Queen Elizabeth II's coronation on a grainy TV at the Maverick Inn, where a live crow presided as a pet.

CHARLIE'S ICE CREAM PARLOR

Teenagers and younger hung out after school at Charlie's Ice Cream Parlor—occupied by the music venue Joyous Lake—which had a jukebox! That's where we heard "All Shook Up" and "Don't be Cruel" for the first time. Sue Mellert was Charlie's stepdaughter, and she could dance. Woodstock librarian D.J. Stern, by the way, was a big fan of Elvis in those days. Meanwhile, Libby Titus and I were enthusiastic consumers of Charlie's special "Pig's Dinner," a gooey concoction of sweets, a predilection that was reflected in our physiques.

The heart went out of old Woodstock when the Seahorse Tavern closed in the 1960s, and the original Deanie's Restaurant (which had started as a diner in a trolley) burned during the 1970s. Although Deanie's reopened at another beautiful location, the ambience just wasn't the same. And although the popular intellectual bartender John Brown made guest appearances now and then, the scene was less ribald than the Seahorse and less homey and the condiments more frugal than when Deanie's was located on the corner of Deming and Mill Hill, in the renovated building now occupied by Fletcher Gallery.

The village (as we called it then) suffered another blow in the late 1970s when the state replaced our bluestone sidewalks with concrete and reconfigured the Village Green, creating an inconvenient protuberance at the intersection of Old Forge and Rock City Roads. Shopkeeper "Just Alan" held his ground, however, so his was the only store that could still boast its durable native sidewalk.

CHRISTMAS SHOPPING

Back to the 1950s. Christmas shopping was best accomplished in Kingston in those days, or so we felt at the age of ten or eleven. Mary Elwyn (she lived in the blue house overlooking the Village Green and had the best view of Santa

Christmas Eve on the Village Green is Woodstock's most established and endearing tradition. Each year, the best-kept secret in town is how Santa will arrive to greet young and old alike.

on Christmas Eve) and I would make a day of it. With great excitement, we'd board the bus for Kingston—unescorted by burdensome parents—and get off at the Crown Street station. Woolworth's was right around the corner! I spent like a sailor on costume jewelry and figurines for everyone on my list. Mary averted her eyes while I chose something for her.

Mary had more discerning taste and sometimes returned to Woodstock with nary a purchase. She had fun anyway. After shopping, we'd drop into a booth at Neko's drugstore and indulge in milkshakes and grilled cheese sandwiches. Then back to Crown Street for a jolly ride home in the dark, hearts brimming with sugarplums and pride. To this day, we reserve one day a year to Christmas shop together. Only now we order cocktails instead of shakes.

ICE SKATING

Four popular skating ponds spring to mind. There was the one since filled in at Andy Lee recreation field, where a kerosene-heated cabin offered respite and hot cocoa. When it snowed at night, we shoveled pathways on the ice while we skated, staring into a dizzying spotlight. There was also Yankeetown Pond in the hamlet of Wittenberg, which I believe is still used by skaters. It was a wildly natural setting, punctuated by beaver dams and shrubby coves. Its grand expanse exceeded the reach of the bonfire that was kept burning on the frozen shore.

There was "Peter's Pond"—Peter Whitehead, that is, son of the Byrdcliffe Art Colony founder Ralph Radcliffe Whitehead—which is now bordered by houses on the south side of Glasco Turnpike across from the western entrance to Upper Byrdcliffe. There were bonfires there, and hot chocolate, too. No spotlights. Finally, there was "Fairyland," a small wooded wetland at Woodstock Estates. Tree trunks green with moss evoked a delicacy that rebuffed human interference. That little habitat is now traversed by a berm conveying sewer pipes to an affordable housing project.

The Broun family skated a lot, as did Virgil Van Wagonen, proprietor (with his wife, Louise) of the Bearsville Market and Feed Store. Virgil introduced me to Streuble Pond in Kinston, which has since been filled in for no good reason. Friends say desperate frogs were hopping down Chandler Drive when the backhoes and bulldozers evicted them from their pond.

THE BEARSVILLE STORE

My parents were friends with Virgil and Louise. Louise was the postmaster, who frequently emerged from behind the mail counter to check out groceries at the cash register. My mother took me with her when she did her weekly food shopping on Fridays. I looked forward to it. Louise was beautiful and very nice to everyone, even kids. So was Virgil. Best of all, they had horses and knew everything there was to know about the noble beasts and lots of other country stuff.

The Van Wagonens accompanied us when we bought our first horse (an oversized, rambunctious, loveable Morgan named Troubadour) and helped hitch him to a buggy for a rare jaunt. They showed us the trails that ran along the Sawkill from the Riding Club on Broadview Road to Bearsville.

Later we bought a sleigh, and my father drove Troubadour, with Mary and me aboard, to town one snowy day. There was no traffic to speak of. The horse stood still by the Village Green while I ran into the News Shop to buy a newspaper. Mary says she'll never forget that day.

CHRISTMAS EVE

Woodstock's most popular tradition, the arrival of the real Santa Claus on the Village Green, started in the 1930s, according to Christmas Eve Committee Chair Harry Castiglione. There's live music, caroling and Santa distributes stockings filled with candy to all children who wait in line. In the 1990s, a menorah was added to the green at the holiday season. This is one Woodstock tradition that's likely to last for a long, long time.

Author's Note: This memoir includes revised, combined versions of articles that also appeared in Ed and Miriam Sanders's periodical, the Woodstock Journal, *1995–2002.*

WOODSTOCK MEETS
THE SIXTIES

By Jeremy Wilber

*E*ditor's Note: *The history of Woodstock is one of transition and change. No change, however, has received more attention or notice than that which occurred in the 1960s. While historians are only now exploring the evolution of what became known as the "Woodstock Generation," the following essay offers a glimpse at how change visited Woodstock in the years prior to 1969 and the Woodstock Festival. Though the festival was eventually moved from Woodstock to Bethel, New York, as promoters found both a lack of "official" support in Woodstock and a suitable site, the town of Woodstock served as a crucial incubator for the spirit, energy and creativity that came to characterize that event. The author, who had a front-row seat at the "revolution" as a bartender at many of Woodstock's legendary watering holes during the sixties, would also go on to serve eight years as Woodstock's town supervisor. (What else would you expect?)*

Golden Ages are generally those times preceding ours by about forty or fifty years, and this is no different for Woodstock's golden age, which occurred during the 1960s.

In 1963, the very first hippie came to town. He called himself Link. Link wore an earring, which might as well have been a grenade the way we all jumped behind the hedges, gasped and shuddered. He grew his hair down to his shoulders. If he could *walk* on his hair we would have been no less fearful. A wispy goatee simmered under his chin and barely sewed his thin lips to his nostrils. We cringed. An odious presence was Link. This Link obviously did not want to build a house. Or renovate a barn into a house. Or have a house with two bathrooms. He wanted to smoke marijuana, drink Yago wine and ravish our daughters. He threw his wishes in our faces by parading himself on our Village Green.

For most of history the Village Green just lay there quiet and revered as any churchyard. It was never fenced, a proscription some town leaders came to lament. A little lane interceded so that carriages of the day could draw up to the front doors of the church to discharge the faithful. Fat maples shaded the grass. The church began sharing its lawn with the town at least a hundred years before, as it slowly came to mark the center of town.

The green's empathy for secular traumas began in the twentieth century, when America fought the great wars. A memorial was placed on the green. Raised brass letters on a thick brass band surrounding the wooden flagpole recalled the names of our fallen. A local ordinance at the time prohibited persons from sitting on the raised flowerbed surrounding the memorial. The ordinance was enforced, at least to the extent that Constable Bucky (or Paul or Clancy, the other retired New York City police officers) could shoo off the memorial sitters on.

Link parked his skinny butt on our memorial like a bee on a daisy. We still had a sensible Constitution in those days, and Clancy and Paul and Bucky could shoo people we didn't like. Link was shooed from one end of town to the other with our unanimous approval. Even remnants of the Byrdcliffe Arts and Crafts Colony that were still alive approved of shooing Link. Shooing Link all over town probably put Bucky, Paul and Clancy prematurely into their graves. Remember, this was pre-Nike. But we soon discovered that as a town we simply lacked the breath for constantly shooing Link.

So to keep from exhausting our constables, our town fathers removed the benches from the Village Green. The idea was to make hippies go sit in hell—or someplace else—and leave the memorial alone. Most of us agree it was probably the worst town board decision ever made when you consider the fuss it kicked up. You'd think we tried to draft Link. You'd think Link had been chained and lashed by us. To look at the wispy, goateed man surrounded by his legion of defenders on the Village Green, some of them our daughters and sons, you'd think the gates of Gethsemane had reopened.

Being a reputed Colony of the Arts complicated our irenic lives. Colonies of the Arts attract Link types, we found out. It has always been so. "To the extent thine real estate interests advertise a Colony of the Arts, so shalt Links clog your Village Green," is apparently etched into ancient stones with other rules about murder and idolatry. The realtor who can figure out how to sell our town as a Colony of the Arts and at the same time NOT attract the

Woodstock Meets the Sixties

Link types will have his or her likeness sculpted onto Overlook Mountain in Mount Rushmore fashion.

What had led up to this infestation of Link?

Initially, we seemed not particularly susceptible. In the late 1950s and early 1960s, cars were so poorly made that dozens of us made livings fixing yours. Some of us worked in factories that once dotted our area. We had some artists and craftsmen, sated but not glutted with success. Our day-in-year-out scratch for livelihood made Woodstock not much different from our neighboring communities, *except* that because of our significant population of second-home owners from New York, we were fed their newspapers and magazines daily, including the *New York Times*, the *Journal American*, the *Herald Tribune*, the *World, Sun and Telegraph*, the *New York Post*, the *Wall Street Journal*, the *Mirror* and the *Daily News*. The communities around Woodstock at the time thought New York papers were written in a foreign language. In a way they were, because the Depression, World War II and war on the Korean peninsula had knocked the mood for big stories out of most of us. Local marriages, church suppers and deaths were our preferred taste for news. We would have been happy with this arrangement forever, but the New Yorkers inhabiting the renovated barns and building houses with two bathrooms had it *their* way. While our neighboring towns elbowed and clawed their way through postwar America, blissfully ignorant of the titanic forces of history enslaving us, we knew just from our glancing at the two-inch headlines in front of the News Shop that the Swedish krona had depreciated .053 percent overnight.

The New York newspapers helped Woodstock's melting pot. When we went to the post office and bumped into the New Yorker who overpaid us to plow his driveway, we would say, "Yessir, the krona, and the next thing you'll know the Swiss franc," like we knew what we were talking about. It sure beat standing there with our tongue hanging out with absolutely nothing to say to the ol' moneybag.

We were not quick to realize the importance of skinny Bob Dylan. Before his electric guitar made Woodstock rich, he used to crash in the Cafe Espresso. At first we thought Bernard Paturel, the demi-Frenchman who owned the Café Espresso ("Café Trotsky," "Café Beatnik," etc.) was too kind for too long to the screechy bard who, Bernard admitted, he couldn't understand. We used to sweat all day putting in second bathrooms so we could pay for a French beer at the Café Espresso, and Bob Dylan didn't even sweep the damn floor for his beer and crumbs, we noticed. He sat on the Espresso patio with Joan Baez and Rambling Jack Elliot and Tom Paxton and other players from the folk music crowd like there wasn't a care in the air.

Woodstock's Village Green. Who needs benches?

But in a year or so we got a hint of his magnetism when it rained beautiful women on our town. Up until then our bohemians and artists and writers had hinted a steady, unobtrusive perfume. Bob Dylan's draw, however, fragranced the valley. If Bob Dylan had sprayed barrels of Chanel #5 from airplanes day and night he could not have more thoroughly sweetened the air. You couldn't drive through the village without getting a serious neckache. Our local gals, who'd gone from Eve until just yesterday looking fine in their calico dresses and none-too-particular coifs, all of a sudden were heaped in books and magazines about the New Woman. They got dolled up and chased off to the Café Espresso, where you'd think sat the king of France. What was worrisome was that our local gals could out drink a Viking. They ruled the barroom floors strewn with unconscious, ill, less capable suburban males and females. On the sidelines taking bets you had Paul Butterfield, Todd Rungren, The Band, Tim Hardin, Van Morrison and every high-priced session man on the East Coast. Bob Dylan himself was an elusive object, but his retinue could have been the cast for *Rape of the Sabines*. God, did this rankle us. To have weathered dipping Susie's pigtails into ink wells until her age of majority, only to see her now in tight jeans and a Paree coif skipping off with some conch-belted musician, and sipping Pernod (and just what the hell was *that?*) in the Café Espresso, rankled sorely. Thank goodness Bob couldn't make love to *all* of them. It cannot be overstated, the anomaly of a small town such as ours simply saturated with beautiful women. We were all Paris deciding around them, and fortunately it was hard to feel rankled all the time when playing such a role.

After Bob Dylan went electric, Woodstock turned green as a dollar. We became engulfed with electric guitars. It changed the face of us. Out went our tailor shop, the bakers, the cobbler, the washing machine seller and the last guy to deliver a bottle of whiskey to your house in a driving blizzard. In came the leather shops, the tie-dye shops, the crafts-from-Asia shops and, of course, the tight jeans shop, which also sells shoes for half the price of Cameroon. Eventually we would knock down one of our nicest old houses for extra parking.

(My two cents on Bob Dylan selling out: The alternative to strapping on an electric guitar was getting into a big hissy fight with Pete Seeger over *who* was the *real* heir to Woody Guthrie. The brawl would have stretched out until now. Think about *that*, ye critics.)

The opening in 1959 of the New York State Thruway cut the joy of visiting us from New York City and New Jersey to a two-hour jaunt instead of the five-hour crawl up 9W that it had been since George Washington. The opening of the Thruway and Bob Dylan's electric guitar encouraged many youthful creeds to move here. Yago wine (the cheapest from Franco's Spain) and marijuana, which by today's measure wouldn't stagger a flea, greased the social intercourse. The legendary Sled Hill Café waxed and waned. The Woodstock Festival, which purveyed a generation's music to the multinational corporations, was named after us. We watched big talents striding from bar to bar in our village, their $200 boots carving treads into our bluestone sidewalks aside the main drag, our Susie at their side.

During this infusion there came more hippies. Some brought a genuine peace and love vibe, some brought a drugs, sex and rock & roll sensibility, some got off the bus and asked us, "Where's Dylan's house; I got something important to tell him." This last type was often shrouded in a dark, glazed expression that by comparison would make a zombie seem vivacious. They all shared a disdain for fashionable footwear, in many cases even forgoing their utility, and the sight of toes creeping from worn uppers became not unusual. There was a lot of cheap housing in those days, and "cheap" is used to describe its condition as well as its rent. Matters finally settled into an *entente*, the town realized there were too many hippies to shoo all over the place and the hippies tolerated the occasional drug bust that always seemed

Following the arrival of Dylan and, later, the notoriety bestowed by the Woodstock Festival (even though it wasn't held in Woodstock), a number of young people had the same idea.

to occur the one night of the year when there wasn't so much as a roach in an ashtray.

Then the cars got better and some factories closed and now there are only four newspapers from New York.

Then came the 1970s and houses with *three* bathrooms and scores of new businesses owned by the hippies that stayed.

Then came disco. Yikes!

Visit us at
www.historypress.net